MW00440230

invite
PRESS

CONFRONTING THE

THIEF
WITHIN

WES OLDS
WITH BONNIE CRANDALL

CONFRONTING THE
THIEF
WITHIN

How I Quit Earning God's
Love and Embraced My
Real Identity

All Scripture quotations, unless otherwise noted, are taken from the *Holy Bible*, New Living Translation, copyright © 1996, 2004, 2015 by Tyndale House Foundation. Used by permission of Tyndale House Publishers, Inc., Carol Stream, Illinois 60188. All rights reserved.

Scripture quotations marked NRSVue are taken from the New Revised Standard Version, Updated Edition. Copyright © 2021 National Council of Churches of Christ in the United States of America. Used by permission. All rights reserved worldwide.

Scripture quotations marked NRSV are taken from the New Revised Standard Version of the Bible, copyright 1989, Division of Christian Education of the National Council of the Churches of Christ in the United States of America. Used by permission. All rights reserved.

Scripture quotations marked NIV are taken from THE HOLY BIBLE, NEW INTERNATIONAL VERSION®, NIV® Copyright © 1973, 1978, 1984, 2011 by Biblica, Inc.™ Used by permission of Zondervan. All rights reserved worldwide.

Scripture quotations marked AMP are taken from the Amplified Bible; Copyright © 2015 by The Lockman Foundation, La Habra, CA 90631. All rights reserved.

Scripture quotations marked KJV are taken from the King James Version of the Bible, which is in public domain.

Scripture quotations marked ESV are taken from The Holy Bible, English Standard Version. ESV® Text Edition: 2016. Copyright © 2001 by Crossway Bibles, a publishing ministry of Good News Publishers.

*For Caleb,
my beloved son.*

CONTENTS

FOREWORD

As a child, I loved to read, and mysteries were my favorite. I started with the Bobbsey Twins, then the Hardy Boys and Nancy Drew. Mystery books offer facts, and then the reader (or writer) is challenged to look beyond the obvious to the unknown that will solve the mystery. As an adult, I discovered that mystery is threaded throughout life. As a Christian, mystery was part of growing into my faith.

I became a professional clinical counselor to help others find their way through the mysteries of their individual lives. I began my counseling practice using tried and true approaches to self-discovery. Cognitive Behavioral Therapy, developed by Aaron T. Beck in the 1960-70s, seemed to make the most sense to me. How we think directs how we behave. How we behave is connected to our thinking. When either our thinking or our behavior harms us, then we need to look more closely at our thoughts and actions in order to make healthier choices. That means change. For me, the most powerful book of change and wholeness is the Bible.

I have long believed that the Bible is one of the most free-ing and impacting *psychology* books available to humanity. It is all about change. It includes all the components for lasting and healing change: forgiveness, unconditional love, wholeness, personal peace, freedom, encouragement. In addition, we are invited by Jesus to "be filled with all of the fullness of God" (Eph 3:19 NRSVue) and to fully embrace the invitation to be-come God's child. The Bible challenges our thoughts and be-haviors. It affirms the power of "renewing of the mind" (Rom 12:2 NRSVue).

While sitting on a park bench in 1998, my eyes fell on a colorful wall mural painted on the side of an old downtown building. My life-changing moment had arrived. COGPOW (Child of God Person of Worth), the term I coined that would come to define my biblical counseling method, found its be-ginning as I stared at that wall. The brightly colored happy mu-ral made me smile. It had been up for a while and some paint was peeling. Underneath the colorful mural was more paint, but it was dark and angry: Graffiti. God encouraged me to see a biblical truth as I began to understand a primary and shared experience of life. All of us come into life like a blank wall. As children, we have little power to determine what others can paint on our *wall*. It can be a beautiful mural or graffiti.

Over the next several years, God continued to drop *aha mo-ments* of new understanding and biblical application into my head. I began to think about how our thinking and responses are formed, and how they can free us or trap us. Being both a clinical counselor and a Christian, I found myself looking to Scripture for confirmation of the mysterious threads of truth that encouraged wholeness. As the stages and understandings of the COGPOW approach were formed and confirmed by Scripture, I was able to observe the freedom and healing it offered my clients. They discovered that they were not only Children Of God, but also Persons Of Worth, two parts of a whole. The Scripture brought answers to the mystery of their lives that unlocked their minds and strengthened their souls.

In following that process, I found I had developed a new method of counseling combining both mind and spirit. This involved developing new images: *the wall, the great commandment, the order of the love, the village, the Smurfs, putting away childish things, claiming your adult authority*, and *choosing to respect God's child.* All are components that emerged as God chose to reveal them. All of these confirm Paul's statement of "the glorious riches of this mystery, which is Christ in you" (Col 1:27 NIV) and reflects the blending of becoming fully mature in peace with God and with yourself.

I have been able to share COGPOW concepts with clergy here in the United States and in parts of Europe and South America. I am always stunned by the response that reflects our deep desire to know, not only that God claims us as God's children, but that this fact alone confirms that we *are* persons of worth. This knowledge brings us wholeness of mind and spirit. And we all long for wholeness.

You are about to meet an amazing person. His name is Wes Olds. He will take you on a life journey of gritty honesty, as he struggles to understand this healing and freeing image of his relationship to God and to himself. His unique journey to discover his identity as a COGPOW in his life will challenge you to a new understanding of mind, body, and spirit in yours. As you read, be open to each application of the COGPOW approach, and examine your own life, seeking out clues to the mystery that is you. Listen to God's whispered encouragement for you to change and become all that you were designed to be. It's part of the adventure that awaits you.

Those who live in Jesus Christ become new creatures. Old things pass away, and a new life begins. You too can claim a clean, new *wall* for you and God to cover in beautiful truths that will put a smile on God's face and on yours, as the wonderful mystery that is you is revealed in living color.

Be blessed and be a blessing.

Bonnie Crandall, MA, LPCC (ret)

ACKNOWLEDGMENTS

Thank you for all of the ways that God has used you to refine this material and my very life!

Dr. Ron Crandall

Dr. Lori Wagner

Dr. Larry Frank

Dr. Jorge Acevedo

The Grace Church Teaching Team

Craig Robertson

Rev. Kevin Griffin

Casey Culbreth

The Nestor's Small Group

The Sanctification Project

Dr. David Thomas

Dr. Brad Olds

Sandy Olds

Becky Olds

And above all, Bonnie Crandall.

CHAPTER ONE:
MY INNER THIEF

Crisis

In the Fall of 2002, my wife Becky and I were the proud parents of a three-year-old son, and we had a new baby boy on the way. We lived in beautiful Central Kentucky and had recently signed a contract on a new house under construction in North Lexington that was large enough for our growing family. Becky worked as a marriage and family therapist with at-risk children and their families. I had just graduated from seminary, was freshly commissioned as a pastor, and had been newly assigned by the leaders of our denomination to bring new life to a dead, 112-year-old, inner-city church. Despite the challenge ahead of me, I was filled with vision and ready to prove myself as a senior pastor at the ripe old age of 32. Life was good!

Within days, I discovered that the journey to *restart* the church was going to be difficult. To my naive surprise, I met with fierce opposition from the remaining members about the changes that they had heard were coming. Even though the average age in the congregation was 82, the remnant of the once-proud church still had enough energy to protect their church from anything new! My first Sunday, a group of women met me at the door and let me know that they *knew* I had been sent to close the church and reopen it with a new name and focus. They informed me that they liked their church just the way it was and would do all they could to make sure my first Sunday was my last one as their pastor. I had been a youth minister in three local churches the previous twelve years, so this was the first time I had been threatened by a group of octogenarians. Sadly, many in the rest of the congregation felt the same way. Their resistance was nothing compared to the challenge that suddenly faced our family.

One day, when I was out of town for a meeting, my wife Becky called me in a panic. "Honey," she said in a broken, frightened voice, "the police are here. A man followed Caleb and me home from the playground and broke into the house." She described how, as she arrived home and entered the house with our toddler son in tow, an armed man barged through the front door. With her mother's instinct and strength, Becky swept up our son with one arm, knocked over the assailant with the other, and fled to our neighbor's house for safety. Within a few weeks, police caught the suspect. Becky identified him in a lineup, and he was arrested.

After that event, which included some nights hiding in a hotel while we waited for the arrest, we tried to return to normal. However, weeks after the attack when we returned to work, peace eluded us. At night, I often slept on the couch with a baseball bat to offer a first line of protection for any other accomplice who might return. Sleep was sporadic.

My ministry remained stressful as attendance at the church only dropped. I faced increased resistance from inside and outside the church over launching a Spanish language service and including Spanish on our church sign. One local business owner opposed our church offering worship in Spanish because, in his mind, it contributed to the problem of illegal immigration in our nation. Our team met with him a number of times to try to come to some understanding, but he only grew more adamant. He began recruiting other business owners and a few nearby residents to oppose the church.

The controversy with this person and his allies grew when, a few weeks later, we opened the church on cold nights for persons experiencing homelessness. Many of these persons were already sleeping in the bushes and alcoves of the property and throughout the neighborhood. We reasoned that it was safer for all involved to invite them into the church basement. Due to neighborhood complaints and the accusation of a zoning violation, the mayor of the city issued our new church a "cease and desist" order, ending our efforts to serve the homeless in that way.

The first night we were forced to close, a man froze to death near the church as he was seeking shelter. The front-page headline in the local newspaper the following day incorrectly reported the events, saying we had refused to open the doors for the man, and he died as a result. I was heartbroken. I foolishly assumed that the media requests I received for interviews about the situation were from friendly reporters who wanted to help our ministry. Instead, I walked right into repeated *gotcha* questions, and the controversy grew. So did my stress. A local expert in public relations called me one day out of the blue and said, "Pastor, stop giving interviews. The press is not your friend!"

As tensions increased at the church, my wife and I faced a new, horrifying challenge at home. During a routine check-up for our soon-to-be-born child, Becky and I learned that our son had severe spina bifida and would not live long after birth. Many nights, I stayed up pleading with God through tears and groans to save my son. Becky did the same. Even though we prayed for a miracle for little Daniel, he died in our arms shortly after being delivered. We were heartbroken. I will never forget coming home after holding our lifeless child at the hospital and then seeing our three-year-old son Caleb waiting by the door, hoping his little brother was going to get to come home. "No, I'm sorry Caleb," I told him. "Daniel went straight to Heaven instead of coming home with us." His reaction was a light of hope in the darkness of the day: Caleb said, "Alright, then. That means he's fixed, Dad! Daniel is in Heaven, and God fixed the hole in his head!" I longed for Caleb's faith. On the day my dad and I had scheduled a visit to buy a new cradle for my son, we bought him a casket instead. We held a graveside service and were blessed by dozens of friends and family who came to support us. As two of my friends sang "I Can Only Imagine," I struggled to imagine how my wife and I were ever going to recover from the tsunami of this loss.

Almost immediately after our son's burial, my grief gave way to furious anger. I had struggled with anxiety for much of my life, and Daniel's death triggered almost daily panic attacks that I expressed in rage. My life seemed as though it was spiraling out of control. I couldn't stop my constant thoughts of worry and fear, which I attempted to mask with more anger. I began to argue with Becky to the point that we slept in separate rooms and avoided each other as much as possible. Soon, our marriage was in serious trouble. When we moved into our new home, the extra bedroom we had planned for our new son served as a constant reminder of our loss. Without ever discussing it, we left the room empty with the door closed, perhaps hoping one day that the bad dream would end. One day I passed by the room and was so overwhelmed with grief that I went into the next room, my home office, and punched the wall, leaving a huge hole in the drywall and cuts all over my hand.

I was mostly angry at myself. These back-to-back-to-back events led me to conclude in my own mind that I was a complete and utter failure. I had the evidence to prove it, too. I could not save my son, protect my wife, or grow my church, all despite my best efforts. My brain got stuck on a repeating loop of these failures. I felt like I had flunked the test at being a good father, husband, and pastor. Who was I if I messed all of this up? I believed I had let everyone down, including God.

My prayers alternated between cries for help and confessions for how I didn't measure up. I made rigorous *to-do* lists in my journal that I was going to try to suddenly accomplish to make the pain go away. I could hardly sleep. I tried taking up smoking cigars at night to distract me from the pain and help me calm down before bed. It left me feeling sick. That didn't work, so I turned to whiskey. That only made me sicker. In my obsessive, self-critical mind, I reasoned I was such a failure that I couldn't even successfully get addicted to something to escape reality.

I tried to hide my alternating rage and despair, especially on Sundays when it came time to deliver a sermon. I honestly wasn't sure where God was, or if God even loved me anymore. Standing up to be a messenger of a grace that I wasn't sure included me was gut-wrenching. One Sunday morning in late November, after I finished trying to preach on the love of God that felt so distant to me, I immediately spiked a 102-degree fever. My heart began to race with panic, and I feared I was having a heart attack. I felt so bad after the service ended that I walked straight out to my car and drove myself to the emergency room. Seven years earlier, I had had aortic valve disease and had to have open-heart surgery to implant an artificial aortic heart valve. That Sunday afternoon, I was convinced my valve had malfunctioned, and I was dying.

When I arrived at the emergency room, in part due to my health history, the attendants and nurses immediately summoned a doctor to examine me. They started an IV, hooked me up to several monitors, and began a series of tests. Thankfully, after several hours, my fever began to subside. The tests showed that everything, including my artificial heart valve, was healthy.

After a few hours, the emergency room doctor came in by himself to my room and closed the curtain. He pulled up a stool next to me and looked me in the eye.

He said, "Reverend Olds, you have a deeper problem than just a fever. I'm going to guess that you're not following your own preaching. Your body is sick because you are pushing yourself too hard. I'm not a pastor, but I can say that if you don't rest, it says in Psalm 23 that God will *make* you 'lie down.'" That doctor could have been a pastor.

He was right. My dad Howard was a pastor, and I grew up under his preaching. A mantra that he often shared in his own sermons went like this: "The body cannot bear what the soul will not resolve." That was my situation. I was *soul sick*. I was exhausted. I was burned out.

Spirit of the living God, fall afresh on me.

A couple of weeks later, as I stood up yet again to try to preach one Sunday morning, I noticed a familiar face in the sea of empty pews. It was my old high school church youth choir director, Bonnie Crandall. She had heard all that had happened to us and had come to show her support. It was good to see her.

Three days later, I received a letter from Bonnie letting me know that she had become a pastoral counselor in the years since I last talked with her. What she wrote next changed my life. She saw through the forged optimistic, faith-filled public face I was trying to put on, and she noticed how badly I was hurting. She saw that, while I was preaching about heaven, I was in my own private hell.

Best of all, she offered to help. Knowing deep down that I was in trouble, I made my first appointment. I was so lost that I was willing to try almost anything that could help me survive.

The next week, I made my way to Bonnie's office for my first counseling session. I had first met Bonnie seventeen years earlier. My father was a pastor in Lexington at the time, and he had hired Bonnie to lead the church's music ministry. Even though I had not spoken with her for over a decade, I felt some relief going to a counselor who knew at least some of my background. I had tried counseling once before, right after my heart surgery, but found it to be of little help for what were, looking back, my first serious signs of depression and anxiety. Instead of engaging in talk-therapy, I tried to hide and ignore those feelings. When my feelings came out, they were expressed only through bouts of anger.

As I sat down on a couch in Bonnie's office for the first time, she gave me a quick recap of her last ten years of education and new calling to counseling. I shared a little of my own journey, keeping the details to a minimum and my emotions strictly guarded. After just a few moments of these pleasantries, she looked intently into my eyes and asked, "Wes, how *are* you?"

As I pondered her question, I suddenly couldn't hold back the tears. To my surprise, I could barely speak. I broke down into one of those ugly crying episodes involving breathing, convulsions, and a lot of tissues. "*How am I?*" I thought to myself. The honest answer was that my life had fallen apart at the moment it was all supposed to come together. As I began to try to share with her my story of loss, frustration, anger, exhaustion, and disappointment, my emotions erupted. Even though I tried, I could not hide from Bonnie. I suppose some part of me felt safe for the first time in a long time. The tears continued. There was no more hiding.

Hiding my true self had become so routine in my life that I often found it hard to say out loud what my soul was feeling. It felt as if admitting my pain would make it more real and that much more painful. As I tried to share with Bonnie a few of my thoughts, I became more upset. I could only squeeze a few words out before catching my breath and forcibly swallowing back the pain. The more I shared, the more I felt utterly exposed and afraid. With each thought that came to my mind, more sweat poured down my furrowed brow and landed on my red cheeks before dripping at last onto my clenched fists.

Mercifully, Bonnie interrupted the increasing avalanche of grief and impending panic attack with a question: "Do you remember the song I used to sing to you all when you were in high school?" she asked. "Yes," as I caught my breath to reply. "Why don't I sing it now?" "Okay," I said, discarding the notion that it was a bit strange that my former choir director-turned-counselor was now going to sing to me as I wept. But anything was better than talking at that moment, so I welcomed her solo.

As I clenched my eyes closed, trying to dam up the wave of pain threatening to overtake the banks of my being, Bonnie's beautiful voice rang out the words of that old song: "Spirit of the Living God":

> Spirit of the living God,
>
> fall afresh on me.
>
> Spirit of the living God,
>
> fall afresh on me.
>
> Melt me, mold me, fill me, use me.
>
> Spirit of the living God, fall afresh on me.[1]

---

1   Daniel Iverson, "Spirit of the Living God," The United Methodist Hymnal (Nashville: The United Methodist Publishing House, 1989), #393. © 1935, 1963 Moody Bible Institute. These lyrics are used throughout this book.

The song became her prayer for me in that moment. As Bonnie sang, my breathing improved, my heart rate lowered, and she reassured me that I was safe and loved. She was there to listen and help. We were not in a rush. The presence of God was with us. I could relax. I could rest.

Something inside of me agreed with the simple lyrics of the song. I thought to myself: *Spirit of the Living God, fall afresh on me! Yes. That's what I need.*

The Search for Identity

I had become a follower of Jesus as a middle-school student and had genuinely entrusted my life to him as my Savior. Throughout my young-adult years and into my twenties, my faith was a vital part of my life. I prayed regularly, read Scripture most days, and kept a prayer journal. I had felt a call from God on my life to enter ministry since I was a boy. After exploring careers in law and education, I accepted a youth ministry position at a local church and enjoyed a dozen years mentoring students and joyfully sharing with them the blessings of a relationship with Jesus.

During my health crisis with aortic valve disease in my mid-twenties, it was my faith that steadied me. God helped me endure two major surgeries, a ten-day hospital stay, and several months of rehabilitation. On the night before my valve replacement surgery, I re-read the entire New Testament and wrote out my last prayer "just in case." I remember experiencing an unexplainable peace and assurance that, if I died, Jesus would care for me and raise me to new life with him.

While I had come to peace in my faith with dying, *living* by faith was my new challenge! Suddenly, after what I perceived to be my complete failure as a husband, father, and pastor, my faith felt incredibly fragile. I was lost. I had been confident to the point of cocky in my twenties, yet all that bravado was now long gone. I was a shell of my previous self. I went through my days wandering through a fog. I felt weak. I worried constantly about what might happen next. To reduce my stress, I tried to make everyone around me happy, but I couldn't. I had only two adjectives to describe what seemed like a million emotions stirring in me: *anger* or, if I was especially vulnerable, *fear*. On top of that, I was so tired. I wondered how in the world I could be this bad off this early in my professional ministry and *adulthood*.

After a few sessions of counseling, I discovered in our conversations that the struggle I was having was so *bone-deep* that the best description for it was a struggle with my very identity. I could not adequately answer the simple question: "Who am I? The tragedies I experienced revealed to me that I was trying each day to amass an imaginary *spiritual-resume* of sorts. Whenever I felt insecure, I would return to my accomplishments and somehow talk myself off the ledge of despair. My journals often contained daily recaps of all the good I had done that day, a sort of prayer-journal-diary and potential-law-brief. These notebooks served as a witness whenever I prosecuted myself for not measuring up. I grew up hearing about an imagined scenario where Christians are put on trial for their faith. The fictitious question was then asked: "Is there enough evidence to convict this person of being a Christian?" My journal served as proof to myself that I was a *real* follower of Jesus, no matter how badly I thought of myself. Closely intertwined were other people's positive opinions about me and my religious performance. Their good opinions served as evidence for good in my ongoing trial against myself.

Bonnie helped me see almost immediately that I was unsuspectingly caught in a dangerous undertow of trying to live and navigate life on the *performance plan.* I lived and ministered to others to prove my worth and earn the right to be accepted and loved. I not only did this for other people; I *performed* for God too. I thought that if I made enough people happy and did enough good things for God, then I too would be worthy of love. None of this was a conscious decision or plan. It was as if a thief had robbed me in the middle of the night, and I was just now recognizing what was missing.

As Bonnie began to probe my thinking, I began to discover that I had unknowingly viewed my salvation and the gift of grace as a "90-Days-Same-As-Cash" deal with God, where the grace that was free to begin with had to be paid back through rigorous self-improvement. The difficulties in my life revealed that my attempts to "be like Jesus" were mainly about *my* effort instead of my simple cooperation with *God's* love. As Bonnie simply and plainly described God's love to me and for me in those first meetings, it was as if I were hearing the news of grace for the first time in my life. I had begun to make connections to things I had heard, and even preached, for years, but they had never completely taken root in my life.

Bonnie explained that people who attempt to live on the performance plan find their identity in external roles. That was certainly true of me. My *titles*—husband, father, son, brother, friend, and pastor—were how I measured my performance and worth in life. The problem was that these roles were often subject to change. They could also be impacted by forces outside of my control. For example, even though I tried, I could not prevent bad things from happening to those I loved. I could not *make* any person like me or my ministry leadership. My roles were not a reliable way to define my identity. My soul needed more than a role to find rest. External titles were no reliable way to answer the question: "Who am I?"

These early days of counseling provided me with the opportunity to begin to examine my inner world, the world of my soul. This is the place where a person's will, passions, and dreams reside. This inner world was designed by God to be the place of our true identity. Bonnie proposed that it was in my soul, not in my roles, that I could find a different identity, one that was stable, consistent, and could sustain me through both the changes and the storms of life. The identity I longed for was deeper and more secure than the one I was cultivating.

For the first time since I was a child, I began seriously to acknowledge the presence (but not yet the needs) of my inner world. I had first discovered this hidden, spiritual nature of myself in elementary school when I sang in a children's choir in church. A line from one of the songs we sang declared that my "soul is the real me, and it's the real you." Just as we all have unique fingerprints and DNA, we each have distinctive gifts, abilities, personality traits, values, and experiences that make us who we are. I began to realize that the needs of my soul had largely been ignored for a very long time.

Suddenly, Jesus' words and ministry began to come to life in new ways. In reading the accounts of Jesus' life, I saw how Jesus cared for people's outward, physical needs: He fed the multitudes, healed the sick, and even raised people from the dead. But I noticed for the first time that there was always something deeper at work. These outward signs were all pointing to the more hidden, inward, and spiritual grace that he came to offer. He once told his disciples that what matters most in life is our inner, spiritual identity: "And what do you benefit if you gain the whole world but lose your own soul?" (Mark 8:36).

This statement described the crossroads I was at in my life. I wanted to excel in my performance, especially in my own evaluation of my relationships. I wasn't after money or fame, yet, gaining the "whole world" for me meant to be approved of and admired by others for my accomplishments. In that pursuit, I had lost my soul. Ironically, even as a pastor, I had forgotten or ignored Jesus' most fundamental teaching: What matters most in life is the health of the soul.

One of my favorite sayings of Jesus comes as he compares himself to the well-intentioned yet misguided religious teachers of his day. The scribes and Pharisees were more concerned with their outward appearances than the health of their souls (see Matt 23:28). Jesus warns his disciples that these Pharisees were behaving essentially as thieves. He then compares them to himself: "The thief comes only to steal and kill and destroy; I have come that they may have life and have it to the full" (John 10:10 NIV).

Since I was a teenager, this was my life-verse. I chose this because I liked the invitation to a full life. If Jesus was the one who was coming to show us how to find that life, I wanted to follow him! Especially since facing death in my mid-twenties, I wanted every moment of my life to be lived to the fullest. The problem was that I ignored the first part of the verse about the thief, and focused only on the *full-life* part.

The voices inside my head were robbing me of Jesus' promise. My addiction to approval was like an inner Pharisee, a habitually, offending thief, stealing, killing, and destroying my soul. I realized that, just as the false teachers had demoralized and criticized people who didn't measure up to their standards, I was doing that to myself! For the first time, I became consciously aware of my own inner, harsh, judge.

Graffiti on the Wall

To help me begin to understand and give language to my inner world, Bonnie introduced me to what she called "The Wall." The very first book of the Bible teaches that each person on planet earth is created in the image of God (Gen 1:27). That included me too. Impressed upon my soul is the imprint of the divine. I am "fearfully and wonderfully made" (Ps 139:14 NRSVue). I am God's poetry, God's "masterpiece" (Eph 2:10).

Bonnie explained that, upon this sacred canvas, we all come into this world like blank walls. God's desire for me was to allow God and others to fill my wall (God's sacred canvas) with images and messages of blessing. To *bless* is to "say good things" to a person. God wants to bless me and, out of the overflow of that gift, for me to bless others.

Yet my soul's *wall* was not simply filled with blessings. A sort of vandalism had occurred. Over God's beautiful murals of blessing on the wall of my soul had been scribbled, angry, harmful, chaotic graffiti. Bonnie went on to describe how, as children, our soul enters the world much like a pure, blank slate or wall. God desires to fill our souls with a lifetime of blessings and goodness. As a child, we are powerless over our wall and dependent on others to write and leave good things on it for our good and God's glory. Some people, even well-intentioned people, and those we rely on to love us, can instead leave graffiti. In my case, I took the spray paint, and in my own pain, I left additional graffiti on the wall of my own soul.

I soon began to see that the tragedies I was experiencing now were not my only losses. I had related pain that was deeply tied to some of the unhealthy messages I had received throughout my life. These were also written on my wall. It was painful enough to struggle through my current loss and disappointment, but I was adding pain to my own suffering. I often returned to selected, unhealthy memories from my past and added to my wall's graffiti. Other people in my life, perhaps out of their own pain, had left destructive messages on the wall of my soul. I latched onto these images and then made my own contributions to the picture that was forming.

To help me grasp this image of my own story, Bonnie offered a list of "graffiti words" that she had encountered in her counseling experience, which she thought could apply to me. They include limiting statements such as:

- You must, mustn't, can, can't

- Always and never

- Woulda, coulda, shoulda

- "Yeah, but . . ." or "What if . . ."

- God may forgive me, but I know I'm still worthless
- If they only knew what a loser I am
- I'm not important
- I'm stupid and/or fat and can't do anything right
- Everyone/no one should like me
- I'm just a [*woman, man, teen, loser, dropout, failure*], so what do you expect!?

Rougher messages included some of these:

- I wish you'd never been born
- Why can't you be more like . . .
- You're just like your . . .
- Do what you're told. You can't think for yourself
- You deserve everything that happened to you. You're nothing
- I am loved as long as I . . .
- Hide my true self
- Do a good job
- Keep the peace
- Make [*insert name*] happy
- Do my devotions
- Keep the family secret
- Never upset anyone . . . don't rock the boat.

The entire last category described me. I was a graffiti ninja. When I was honest, I thought of myself worthy of others' love and God's love only as long as I kept up appearances, did my best, kept the peace, made others happy, did my devotions, kept my family struggles a secret, and never made anyone else upset. As I began to name these previously unspoken messages, I suddenly realized why I was so tired. This was an exhausting way to live!

I added to Bonnie's list some of my own self-diminishing and self-bullying phrases. I spoke harshly to myself with lies such as

- "Wes, you are only kidding yourself that you could make a difference . . . or ever change . . . or really be forgiven . . ."
- "Wes, this is as good as you get. This broken person is all you'll ever be."

These and other disparaging mantras were like inner thieves who came to steal, kill, and destroy my identity. They had stolen from me the abundant, whole life that Jesus freely offered to me. The Jesus I heard about as a kid and read about in the Bible was compassionate and kind to the hurting. But somehow the thieves in my mind stole that gift from me. I felt alone. God had not abandoned me; I had abandoned myself.

As my losses mounted, I doubled down on my efforts to prove myself worthy of love. I had always been stubborn and determined. I could usually power through a challenge when I set my mind to it. This time, however, I was not succeeding, no matter what I tried.

Day after day, I constantly criticized myself for not measuring up. I shared with a close friend some of the inner conversation that was taking place inside my head, and he was stunned. He responded, "Wow, Wes, I can't imagine you saying those things to your worst enemy." But I did. I was my own worst enemy.

As I began to recognize the graffiti on the wall of my soul, I was more desperate than ever to find out "who I was." To begin answering this question, Bonnie encouraged me to look, not within or around, but to "look up" to God. One day, Bonnie said, "Wes, what defines you is that God loves you. It is that simple." She continued, "We can't do anything else until we decide who we are going to be. *Being* is a priority for our soul's health. No matter what we do, our identity emerges from our being." My fundamental identity needed to come from God.

My Fundamental Identity: Loved by God

Bonnie taught me that, as I began to claim my identity in God's love, God would help me erase the graffiti on my wall. It was going to be a long journey. I wrote in my journal a few months into counseling this prayer of surrender:

> I am tired, Lord. Tired of dealing with all the pressures. My own home needs a Savior, and clearly, I'm not it. I am afraid. I don't want to lose any more. I cannot bear another death or tragedy. It hurts to be real. It hurts to be in this world. Help!

One of the starting points for my counseling was not to claim my power, but in my powerlessness to claim my own value. To help me, Bonnie began with the basics of faith. Each week, as I shared what seemed to be the latest news in the unraveling of my life, she would repeatedly remind me of this truth: *I am loved by God.* This was what she called a "core statement," something I could "claim" as my own. Claiming God's unconditional love would be the way that I could begin to claim my own value. Instead of starting with other people's opinions of me or my own self-evaluation, Bonnie urged me to begin with God's love.

This was the first sign of hope in my therapy. Despite all my perceived failures and all my self-criticism, I was beginning to sense that . . . *maybe, just maybe* . . . I was loved by God. My *wall* still said otherwise. But I grew to realize that many of those were lies, old messages that God wanted to erase and rewrite. Bonnie helped me return to the simple and profound truth that God's love is a gift, and it was for me.

Since I had a deep interest in the Bible and was responsible for preaching every seven days, Bonnie often used verses of Scripture to reinforce her encouragement of me. She taught that God gives the Holy Spirit to be constantly present in my life, wooing me and guiding me back to God's love. In my own study, I took comfort in these words from Romans:

> The Spirit you received does not make you slaves, so that you live in fear again; rather, the Spirit you received brought about your adoption to sonship. And by him, we cry, "*Abba*, Father." The Spirit himself testifies with our spirit that we are God's children. (Rom 8:15-16 NIV)

The apostle and early church leader named Paul wrote these words. I wanted what he had! Paul writes with an assurance and confidence in God's love that I longed for in my own life. Whether Paul was in prison, shipwrecked, writing most of the New Testament, preaching to thousands, or running for his life, Paul knew who he was. When he found himself fearful and alone, the Holy Spirit reminded Paul that he was Abba's child. *Abba* is a tender, personal word for father or daddy, even in Jerusalem today. When I visited there many years ago, I could hear little children calling out for their fathers, saying "Abba."

I was beginning to hear with new ears that I was Abba's child! This was my true, inner, lasting identity. My core identity was not *husband, father, son, brother, uncle, cousin,* or even *pastor.* It was not *loser, failure,* or *disappointment* either. I was Abba's child.

This verse from John was one I had read in my Bible countless times, but until that season, I had missed the importance of it:

> But to as many as did receive *and* welcome Him, He gave the right [the authority, the privilege] to become children of God, *that is,* to those who believe in (adhere to, trust in, and rely on) His name. (John 1:12 AMP)

This was all about grace. All those years before I started counseling, I had been looking to find or to try to *earn* an identity. All the while I had missed that *my identity was a gift to receive, not a status to achieve!*

Bonnie had a phrase for this God-given identity. She called it COGPOW, which stands for *Child of God Person of Worth.* Bonnie explained that there is no *and* and no comma between the phrases because a Child of God *is* a Person of Worth.

This phrase immediately lodged deeply in my soul. It was like a missing piece I had been searching for my entire life: COGPOW. Bonnie said this truth was "my home." From that day forward, I began to claim that identity as my own. The self-criticism remained, but now a new thought entered the conversations taking place in my head: Wes is a COGPOW. Just one good thought was enough to bring a ray of hope. For such a long time, I didn't know this gift of being a COGPOW. I served God, but I wasn't a son. I was a preacher of the good news without embracing the good news that I am a Child of God Person of Worth. I began to wonder, "Have I found my identity at last?" That first week Bonnie shared the phrase with me, I repeated it to myself hundreds of times: "Wes, you are a COGPOW." Bonnie soon instituted a new rule: "Wes, do not speak harshly to a COGPOW, especially if it is yourself!"

I wasn't very good at this rule. I did continue to speak harshly to myself. And, honestly, my outward circumstances did not change much at that point. Becky and I were still fighting. In fact, her grief over losing Daniel was just beginning to emerge. I desperately wanted to *fix* her, even though I had my own loss to deal with. My guilt remained for not being present to protect my family from the attack. My church continued to struggle. I was still angry, anxious, and often depressed. I was still looking to others for approval. On top of that, my grandfather died of cancer. After five years of remission, my father's own cancer returned. Day to day life was a struggle for me. Many mornings I simply wanted to bury myself in my covers and avoid the day. Everything was just hard.

What kept me going was that I had a little bit of hope. It was just enough to keep moving. In the uncertainty of every day, I would at some point remember that I was a COGPOW. As I thought about this more and more, I realized that this was a no-strings-attached title. I was a COGPOW no matter what. For the first time in my life, I considered that God's love is available to me regardless of my faults and failures. I soon reasoned that, even if my marriage ended, God's love would remain. Even if I wasn't a perfect father, my Heavenly Father loved me. Even if I failed as a pastor, God loved me. Even if my dad died of cancer, God loved me. Even if I was a second-rate, half-hearted, disobedient, failure as a Christian, God's love would not leave me. The Spirit of the Living God began to fall afresh on me.

While much remained the same, the one thing that immediately changed was my preaching. Even as I struggled each day in so many ways, I found a kindred soul in history. I am named after a preacher named John Wesley. He was once doubting his faith so much that he asked a friend how in the world he could possibly continue to preach. His friend replied: "Preach faith till you have it; and then, because you have it, you will preach faith."[2] This is what I decided to do. I would preach faith until I had it. I reasoned that there were no crowds of people coming to my church anyway, so at least my sermons should benefit me!

As I began to preach on the gift of grace, I started using the phrase COGPOW in my sermons. On the first Sunday I shared the phrase, a new person in our church came up to me and whispered with a laugh, "I think we might see the same counselor!" We quietly compared notes and agreed to pray for each other. Even better, she came back the next week with her husband and a friend!

Each week, on Sundays, I began to unpack Bonnie's defining values. I suddenly had news to share. Not just any news,

---

2 "Wesley's Four Resolutions," *Journal of John Wesley*, accessed 9/16/2022, https://www.ccel.org/ccel/wesley/journal.vi.ii.xi.html.

but *good news*. I often would leave Bonnie's office and go immediately to my office to study the Bible. In part, it was to get ready for the next sermon, but it was really for me.

In one of my discoveries, I realized that this concept of COGPOW was how I saw Jesus anchor his own identity. In the biographies of Jesus' life, Jesus begins his public ministry by coming to his cousin, John the Baptizer, to be baptized. But when Jesus comes to be baptized, he doesn't come because he needs cleansing from sin. I began to see this from a new perspective, the human side of Jesus' life. I began to wonder, what if, before Jesus entered the next three years of his ministry, including all the controversy of being a public figure and the private temptations of the devil, Jesus needed God to say, in essence, "You are a COGPOW."

That's what happens at Jesus' baptism:

> At that time Jesus came from Nazareth in Galilee and was baptized by John in the Jordan. Just as Jesus was coming up out of the water, he saw heaven being torn open and the Spirit descending on him like a dove. And a voice came from heaven: "You are my Son, whom I love; with you I am well pleased." (Mark 1:9-11 NIV)

God in all divine fullness—Father, Son, and Holy Spirit—are present in this one defining moment. The first thing that Jesus and the crowd hears is a voice from heaven calling out, "You are my son, whom I love; I am well pleased with you."

I'm sure the crowd needed to know that the long-awaited Messiah had arrived. But suddenly, in my life, I started to wonder if God spoke these words for Jesus to hear. Maybe Jesus, since he was human like me, needed to have the issue of his identity settled before stepping out into ministry.

What was most compelling to me about the scene of Jesus' baptism and blessing is *when* it occurs. Since I had been attempting to build a list of accomplishments that I thought would make me worthy of love and form my identity, Jesus' lack of noteworthy spiritual accomplishments stood out to me. In fact, with my new lens of looking at the life of Jesus, it seems that, for three decades, he stayed home with his mother Mary and his brothers and sisters. Joseph had presumably passed away, and Jesus took over responsibilities in helping provide for them. I never felt comfortable pointing this out in Sunday school, but now I could not skip the fact that Jesus was thirty years old and lived with his mom!

Not only that, but up to this point, Jesus hadn't yet done anything that would change history. There were no records of him doing miracles, no teaching, no acts of compassion, no healing, no challenging of religious authorities, or any other headlines. He did spend that day at the temple when he was a young teen, causing his parents some anxiety and stress; but at the time of his baptism, he had zero disciples or crowds following him. There was no cross, no suffering, no resurrection from the dead, no Great Commission. Nothing. At age 30, Jesus' resumé was pretty empty! Yet he had God's full and complete blessing.

I was starting to realize that, before I ever did anything for God, God still loved me, delighted over me, and called me God's own son. I wrote these reminders to myself:

- Wes, there is nothing you have ever done that makes God love you less.

- Wes, there is nothing you can do to make God love you more.

- Wes, there is no need to try to earn God's love.

Before seeing Bonnie, I had somehow picked up a false message that God's love had to be earned. I had to be "a good boy" and "good father," a "good friend, church member, pastor, Bible-reader . . ." and much more; then God would love me. I now realized this was not true. God already loved me.

As I started thinking in new ways that I was, perhaps, a Child of God Person of Worth, I began to dream about what it would be like to be fully known, accepted, and loved by God. I wondered what that life could be like compared to what I was experiencing now.

In those first weeks seeing Bonnie, I began to consider new images of God. Instead of raging against me or condemning me, I imagined God to be a tender father who gently wraps his arms around me and says, "I love you. You are my beloved. With you, I am well pleased. You bring me joy." Into my brokenness, God wanted to bring healing. I could now imagine God saying, "Now, let's see if together we can get to a better place and vanquish those *thieves* that keep you from fully experiencing my love."

The truth was, I had lots of thieves.

Author Henry Nouwen says, "We are the Beloved. We are intimately loved long before our parents, teachers, spouses, children, and friends loved or wounded us. That is the truth of our lives."[3]

---

3   Henri Nouwen, *Life of the Beloved* (New York, NY: Crossroad, 1992, 2002), 36.

CHAPTER TWO:
THE VILLAGE

Spirit of the living God, fall afresh on me.
Melt me . . .

One day further along in our conversations, I came into Bonnie's office very frustrated. I had welcomed the news a few months prior of being a COGPOW. I took to that message like a duck takes to water! What a joy it was to know that I am loved by God and that God's love alone gives me worth! I began to give myself a small measure of grace, and my soul welcomed the break from the constant self-bullying that had been going on for years. But the brief interludes of peace that I had started to experience were under constant interruption by my need to make other people happy, fix them, or control them, so that their behavior didn't make me afraid or angry. This was impossible, and so all day, every day, people around me were driving me crazy. I lived in constant fear that I would disappoint someone. Any criticism sent me spiraling back down the black hole of self-criticism.

The Spirit of the Living God had fallen afresh on me with the news that I was loved by God. I found that I could momentarily live in the security I found in that love and the identity of being a COGPOW. For a time, I thought this alone would solve all my problems and return me to my old, more confident, self. But it didn't. I still was not healed.

Bonnie reminded me that living day-to-day life as a COGPOW was a journey of change, and that change takes time. "The only way we change is through crisis and disequilibrium," she explained. "Part of growing is struggle," pointing me back to the next words of the song: "Melt me, mold me, fill me, use me." First, the Spirit of the Living God needed my permission to "melt me." My relational troubles were the perfect place to begin: "Melt me . . ."

The process of preparing gold for sale in the market involves applying pressure and extreme heat, which melts the gold to separate it from all impurities. In much the same way, the Spirit of the Living God would use my broken relational world to begin to melt away impurities in my soul, things such as pride, fear, and codependency.

My trouble with relationships started in my home, where it was harder to hide my true self. My frustration with things at home flowed freely into all my relationships. I felt that, if I could change my life at home, everything else might fall better into place. So, as I sat down in my familiar spot in Bonnie's office one day, I tried to set the agenda for our conversation:

"Bonnie, I want to talk with you today about how I can change my wife, Becky." I was serious.

She replied, "Oh you do?" with a curious look before her big smile broke through along with her boisterous laugh. "Why would you want to talk about Becky today, especially since she's not even here?" she asked.

Feeling defensive, I made my case. "Well, my wife is still a wreck after our son's death. We are constantly on each other's nerves and bickering. We sleep in separate parts of the house. I keep inviting her to join me here in counseling, but she won't come. Since she won't come, I guess I'm just going to need to know how to change her myself."

After probing the depths of my "stinking-thinking," Bonnie's countenance turned serious. "Wes," she explained, "Becky is not in the room, so we are not going to talk about her. You are here. Let's talk about you and your anger toward her and others." My furrowed brow registered my non-verbal disappointment at Bonnie's reply. I noticed that as my silent rebuttal landed its mark, Bonnie doubled down.

"Wes, let me ask you a question: If Jesus took your place in your marriage, would your household be different? Would it be better or worse?"

I protested at the question, refusing at first to answer. Usually, people I tried to argue with gave up faster than Bonnie did. I let the silence again express my disapproval at the question.

Bonnie embraced the quiet for a long time. She then said, "I'm curious why you won't answer the question. It's simple. If

Jesus took your place and Becky never changed, would things be better or worse in your household?"

"Okay, I'll play along," I said. "If Jesus *himself* took my place as Becky's husband, then yes, things may be a little better," I confessed.

"Well, Wes, let me give you some news. You are not yet Jesus." She paused to let that news settle in my soul a bit.

Then she continued: "I have an idea: Why don't you work on yourself first, and then you can turn your attention to Becky."

Her words shocked me to clarity. To this day, I'm grateful for her relentless desire to cut through my defensiveness. At that time in my life, my raging insecurities caused me to try to win every argument and protect myself with layers of false bravado and pride.

Bonnie was right, I was the one who needed changing, not Becky . . . not anyone else. The old hymn says it best:

> It's me, it's me, O Lord,
> standing in the need of prayer.
> Not my brother, not my sister,
> but it's me, O Lord,
> standing in the need of prayer.[4]

As the "Spirit of the Living God" began to "fall afresh on me," God would gently, kindly, and yet firmly need to "melt me" the way a goldsmith might remove the dross from gold (see Prov 25:4), or the way a sculptor might cut away excess rock to reveal a figure.

---

4   African American Spiritual, "It's Me, It's Me O Lord," *The United Methodist Hymnal* (Nashville: The United Methodist Publishing House, 1989), #352.

A few years ago, my wife and I had the privilege of visiting Florence, Italy, to see the great artist Michelangelo's work. While we were thrilled to see the famous statue of David, what was most meaningful to us were nearby: four unfinished statues referred to as "The Prisoners" or "The Slaves." These four figures represented a person seemingly trying to break free from a prison of rock. Our guide informed us that Michelangelo used his chisel with the gentleness of a brush. She told us, in essence, what one travel resource says about these four statues:

> Michelangelo believed the sculptor was a tool of God, not creating but simply revealing the powerful figures already contained in the marble. Michelangelo's task was only to chip away the excess, to reveal. Michelangelo is famous for saying that he worked to liberate the forms imprisoned in the marble. He saw his job as simply removing what was extraneous.[5]

As our guide described this famous artist's approach to his work, I couldn't help but see the parallels of how God seemingly does God's work with me. God uses that divine chisel with the gentleness of a brush, chipping away and liberating those parts of me that have become imprisoned. What a beautiful image!

I've often heard that before a person can learn something new, that person first needs to unlearn something old. That was certainly my case in my next step of healing.

As the weeks gave way to months sitting in that office, it became clear to me that, before I could fully embrace the new

---

5   "Michelangelo's Prisoners or Slaves," Accademia.org: Guide to the Accademia Gallery in Florence, accessed 9/11/2022, https://www.accademia.org/explore-museum/artworks/michelangelos-prisoners-slaves/.

life as a COGPOW, old patterns of thinking needed to be re-placed with something new. Bonnie's guidance involved *un-learning* two soul-deep convictions and welcoming something new from God into my life.

The first misunderstanding in my life involved misconceptions about God's Word and God's love. The second involved how I understood myself and my thought patterns. In the twenty years since my discovery, I've met with dozens of people who shared the same two misunderstandings that I had. Sadly, like me, they too have suffered because of it.

Relationships and the Order of God's Love

First, I had a profound misunderstanding of what Jesus taught as the order of God's love. As long as my understanding of Jesus' teaching and the gift of God's love remained out of order, my life would remain in disorder. Because I had not recognized the free gift of God's love, I spent many years of my life secretly and simply trying to make other people happy. In the months leading up to my counseling, I had failed miserably.

I've since come to discover that, even on my best days, relationships are difficult. In my life, relationships often serve as a mirror, revealing my true self. My dad used to say that, in life, we are like porcupines huddled together in a snowstorm. We need each other to stay warm and survive, but we sure are a prickly bunch! Relationships require lots of grace because they are complex. Surprisingly, we often minimize the complexity of relating healthily to one another.

When you encounter a complicated situation, have you ever heard the statement: "Well, it's not rocket science"?

When it comes to relationships, rocket science is easy by comparison. A news story in my adopted home state of Florida reveals just how tough relationships are for even the most educated and celebrated people.

In 2007, Dr. Lisa Nowak, a distinguished and decorated NASA astronaut, was arrested for assault and attempted kidnapping of a woman who got involved with the man Nowak was having an affair with. Nowak, a former Space Shuttle astronaut and International Space Station scientist, drove across the continental United States wearing a space-diaper because she was in such a hurry to confront the woman. As I read the account of this twisted tale of relational catastrophe, I was stunned to learn Nowak's educational background. Do you want to guess what her doctorate degree was in: *Rocket Science!* That's right, rocket science!

Relationships are not rocket science. They are *more* complicated! This is why, as Children of God Persons of Worth, we need God's help in navigating our relational world.

Jesus knew the complexity of relationships, and so he taught his disciples that healthy relationships begin, not with another person, but with God. By our own power, we don't have enough fuel to make our relationships fly.

One day, Jesus shared with his disciples the greatest command in all of Scripture. As recorded for us in Mark 12:30-31 (NIV), Jesus says,

> "Love the Lord your God with all your heart and with all your soul and with all your mind and with all your strength." The second is this: "Love your neighbor as yourself." There is no commandment greater than these.

As Bonnie shared these words, part of me was honestly hoping that we would move along soon, so I could learn how to fix my wife. I had heard these words since I was a child. I even got a sticker for memorizing this verse in first-grade Sunday school. Now, as I sat with Bonnie, I had earned a Master of Divinity and was a vetted, commissioned, and credentialed pastor. My title was *Reverend*. I knew this, right? The answer was no. I did not. Not in my heart. Somehow, I had completely missed the simplest detail of Jesus' most well-known command.

Jesus says that healthy relationships begin first with our relationship with God, and then we let God's love flow into our lives. Then (and only then) do we let that love flow into our relationships with our neighbors. Bonnie suggested I think of it this way:

As a COGPOW,

- I love God

- I love myself

- I love my neighbors

God is first, I am second, others are third. Why? Well, I can't give what I *ain't* got. That's bad grammar but true in relationships. We cannot love and value another person if we do not love and value ourselves. If we try, we end up loving our neighbor as we wish we could love ourselves or the way we wish other people loved us.

For some reason, I always thought that, in Jesus' teaching, I was in third position. My misunderstanding was that I was to love God with all that I have, then love everyone else with all that I have, then whatever was leftover was for me.

Perhaps I came at it honestly. When I was growing up in church, I once (before meeting Bonnie) sang in the "JOY Choir." What did J.O.Y. stand for? It stood first for <u>Jesus</u>, then for <u>Others</u>, and then last . . . *and certainly least* . . . <u>You</u>. Some of the most celebrated followers of Jesus in my life were constantly running to rescue another soul from some emergency or another, rarely if ever stopping to rest in the love God longs to share. The local churches I was a part of and even worked at exalted those who were *faithful* volunteers who went *above and beyond*, always with the caveat that, of course, they did it all for the glory of God.

I once saw a cartoon with a disheveled man in a strait jacket being led out of the front doors of a church by four men in medical scrubs. A waiting white van sat nearby with the back doors open and ready. A pastor and another leader stood to the side of the scene and with a reluctant sigh, the pastor said, "We are sure going to miss Larry; he was one of our church's best volunteers!"

As I grew up in church, the commandment of Sabbath was often overlooked. It was in my house anyway. My father was a pastor, and so Sundays were busy. When I became a pastor, I followed in Dad's footsteps. I overbooked my schedule and ministry calendars all week and worked on Sunday. I took on too many things at once, all in the name of a lofty and laudable mission to "reach the world." In these ways, I found the local church can be an incubator for growing people with Christian-codependency and poor boundaries. In my own mind, I was one of the best. Since I was working "for the Lord," I always had to work *more*. After all, the more I did, the more accolades I received. My denominational supervisors applauded my 110 percent effort.

One day, I was so tired from all the conflict at home, at church, and with the community leaders that I confessed my exhaustion to Bonnie with this statement: "Bonnie, in my local church, as the pastor, and in every other part of my life, I feel like my work is never done." Bonnie asked me the "Dr. Phil" question: "Wes, how's that working for you?" "Terrible!" I said. I then became angry: "I mean, Bonnie, I feel like I'm killing myself for all these other people, and some of them don't even care! It's not just church; I feel this way at home too. I can't do anything right to help Becky. No matter what I do, it is never enough."

In the spirit of Michelangelo, Bonnie brought out her *chisel* with this question: "Wes, Jesus already died on the cross for all the people in your church, your community, and your family. So, I have to ask: Why are you killing yourself? Was Jesus' sacrifice not enough? Do you need to somehow add to it?"

I knew better than to say yes, even though I desperately wanted to. The truth was, I was somehow trying to be a savior, but not for any righteous motive. At the end of the day, I loved others so feverishly only because I longed to feel loved myself. Yet, I did not.

I was attempting to love others when I didn't accept that I was loved and didn't love myself. I was trying to love other people while at the same time I thought myself unlovable. No matter how I tried, that equation simply would not add up. One late night journal entry captured my frustration with myself on January 5, 2003:

Another fight. Now I'm angry. Somehow, Becky sleeps. I hate myself when I'm like this. I am the worst person . . . and now I am at my worst. I am the person I never wanted to be. Yes, this is me, right now. This is real. Ugh. I am trying so hard. It's never enough. Soon, somehow, I've got to make peace with all this. I'm at a loss. I'm over my head. Help!

As I limped along with my poor self-image—carrying around bags full of guilt, living my days hurried and upset—loving others was difficult. The more I bullied myself, the more I was inclined to bully others. As long as I thought I was unworthy of love, I would view others the same way. Jesus says, "For the mouth speaks what the heart is full of" (Luke 6:45). It was no wonder that my relationships were a mess. The *mess* flowed from my own heart.

I soon realized that only when I accepted God's acceptance of me would I be empowered to extend God's acceptance to others. Only when I let God love me could God's love flow through me to others. I needed to get this order straight: Love God, then myself, then others. Each of these last two are modeled on how God loves.

To *love myself* simply meant to know and claim that what God says about me is true. It was not to assert some sort of superiority over others. In fact, God gives equal value to every soul on planet earth. I needed to value myself the way God values me. My problem was that I was not telling myself the truth about God's love. Deliverance from these lies would come only as I confronted myself with enough truth that they no longer held power over me and my soul. As I realized the depth of my problem, I also recognized that this was not going to be a one-time fix. The journey forward was going to involve identifying these lies and allowing God's truth to set me free. The new goal Bonnie suggested I live for, throughout this journey and the rest of my life, was living *to please the heart of God*.

Pleasing the heart of God would involve all aspects of life, not just "doing things for God" or completing a checklist of accomplishments. Some days, it could please the heart of God when I care for other people in a variety of ways. But other days, it could please the heart of God when I simply care for and value the soul that lives within me. This was not a linear, transactional relationship with God in which I would take a few moments in the morning for a devotion and then go about my day on my own strength. As Bonnie and I visited together, I began to recognize God's wish for me, a life full of devotion, living for one thing: pleasing God's heart. The idea of pleasing the heart of God brought together all my relationships and activities under one goal. Instead of a "million things to do," I had one. Instead of "making everyone happy," I had only God to please.

Jesus modeled this in his life. God's love was the *glue* that held him together. Loving God, self, and others wasn't a *checklist* but a soul-deep identity that gave Jesus great freedom no matter his circumstances.

One way I began thinking of living as a COGPOW was to think daily about loving God, self, and others as something to hold securely in tension, with Jesus' help. I began to view God's order of love this way:

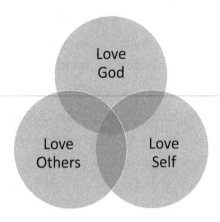

The greatest command was a package deal, bound together by one word: *Love*. I needed all three parts of Jesus' command working together at once. My biggest problem was that I had almost completely neglected the second part of God's order: "loving self." I looked at Jesus' life and teaching through a very cloudy lens. In my distorted view, Jesus' commands to "lay down my life" or "deny myself" reinforced in me more people-pleasing behavior. I thought I was denying myself in my compulsive habits of people-pleasing and lack of boundaries. That was not at all what Jesus had in mind. That emerged out of my poor self-image, not the identity of being a COGPOW. Jesus had boundaries and limits. All my over-functioning in relationships were only encouraged as I further misunderstood how Jesus lived his life out of an overflow of God's love for him.

All three parts of Jesus' command needed to become essential for me:

- If I only "love God" and "love self"—I can be judgmental, a narcissist, or a "know it all."

- If I only "love God and "love others"—I can be a "people pleaser" or a martyr. I can easily become enmeshed in other people's opinions, wants, and needs.

- If I only "love others" and love myself"—then I may think of myself as a "good person." But here's the pitfall: If I decide I am a good person apart from God, then there is nobody greater than myself to determine my very understanding of what *goodness* is. When Jesus enters the picture, the word *good* takes on a whole new meaning!

Living fully into my identity as a COGPOW means all three dynamics of loving God, self, and others under the singular focus of living to please the heart of God alone. One of the things I always admired about Paul was that he was free from the opinions of others. In Galatians 1:10, he says this: "Obviously, I'm not trying to win the approval of people, but of God. If pleasing people were my goal, I would not be Christ's servant."

Again, this preaches well but lives hard. I left Bonnie's office several times thinking to myself, "I understand now! I've got this! I'll just love God and live to please his heart, and all will be better." Sometimes within hours, however, I would be back to my angry self.

At that time, the primary approval I was living for was the approval of my wife Becky. I wanted so much to please her and make her happy. After all, in a twisted way, I felt like I owed her, since I didn't protect her from the home invasion, and I was helpless when our son died. We had both grown up in homes with marital conflict, and each of us had promised the other early in our relationship that "that would never be us!" We were so wrong.

As I began to apply this new wisdom I was finding, I knew I needed to reorder my life to match the order of God's love. I needed to begin with the relationship that was troubling me the most: the one with my wife Becky. To begin to live to please the heart of God meant that I would need to stop making it my secret chief goal of living to please Becky above all else, or anyone else. I don't think I ever had the courage to tell Bonnie out loud, but I honestly longed for Becky's approval more than I did God's. The conflict between us was impacting everything else. The very idea of not trying to *fix* her and *make* her happy seemed counterintuitive to me. I often debated this in my mind and concluded how noble I was to put my wife as number one on my list in my life, even though this was clearly not working.

One day, after meeting with Bonnie, I wrote this question in my journal: "What or who is it that I am stressed the most about?" I put next to it this answer: "My relationship with Becky." Bonnie explained that my marriage fit into the order of God's love this way: Becky was my first neighbor. So, to be in alignment and in order with God's love, Becky would need to move out of the top spot. I needed to love God first, recognize God's love for me, and then and only then could I be free to love Becky. That was not the order I had. In my head, I sought to love Becky first, then love God, then love myself. Living out my new identity as a COGPOW meant God had to replace my wife as my chief audience, the one I was living to please.

I needed to secure my identity in God's love. Before I could ever engage in a conversation with Becky, I had to stop bullying myself and rest in God's love for me, not in the credentials I earned through my religious performance or as a model husband. I needed and could receive grace, just like anyone else on planet earth.

I also needed forgiveness. Bonnie shared that God's forgiveness is a freedom from unmet expectations and from wounds of the past. That certainly applied to me! I had huge expectations for myself and needed forgiveness. More than that, I needed to forgive myself. My past was present with me all the time. I had gotten stuck replaying scenes of my failures over and over again in my mind. It was like driving around all day in a cul-de-sac. I couldn't escape.

I needed God's forgiveness. God's forgiveness could help me remember those events in a new way that was encouraging instead of demeaning. Instead of rehearsing my failures, I began to alter my thoughts about my memories. I remembered those times of failure as, not faults but reminders of God's love that never quit on me. My self-forgiveness did not happen in some dramatic moment. Instead, it soaked into my soul slowly over the course of several months. While not fast, this new start was empowering.

Speaking of power, living as a COGPOW who rested in God's love meant I needed to start accepting the power that God had entrusted to me. For example, I began to realize that I was responsible for my own feelings, actions, and behavior. Since I was a Child of God Person of Worth, I had no right to verbally abuse myself in my own mind. I had no right to do that to someone else, either. I may not have power over all my circumstances, but God had given me power over my responses. I began to claim some measure of the authority that was within me.

Bonnie suggested that Becky and I were each reacting from a common and even predictable pattern of communication even before we spoke. Bonnie took out a sheet of paper and wrote it out for me. A healthy pattern of communication flows like this:

A	B	C	D	E
Situation	Thinking	Feeling	Thinking	Action

There is a situation that takes place (A). I think about it (B). That thinking leads to a feeling (C). That feeling leads to more thinking (D). At last, I can take some appropriate, *well thought out* action (E). The power, Bonnie suggested, was in B and D, the thinking stages of this pattern.[6]

I discovered that in my communication with Becky, I would skip steps B and D. Instead of thinking, I would jump from the situation to a feeling and then quickly to an action. By not stopping to think, I was guilty of what she called "ACE" communication. Here's an example:

- Some situation (A) occurred in our marriage, maybe as mundane as the need to pay a bill.

- I took that situation and often didn't think. Instead, I jumped to feelings (C), usually of fear or anger. The reaction sounded like this: "We don't have enough money for this. I thought she already paid our bills!" or,

---

6   The ABCDE Model is a simple mnemonic developed by Albert Ellis in the field of rational-emotive behavioral therapy that helps people mentally work through a reflection process to consider if they want or need to change their thinking and therefore their behavior around some emotions. Referred to as rational-emotive behavior therapy, it works to target dysfunctional thoughts and beliefs.

"Why can't I provide better for my family?" "Why can't I get it together?" or "She doesn't care about me."

- Then I would take action (E), usually by opening my mouth! "Becky, I've had it with these late bills! I'm done talking with you about this!"

Bonnie gently but correctly assessed my communication and my life this way: "Wes, your habit is to keep yourself in turmoil." ACE communication was a dangerous pattern for me. "But now," she said, "as a COGPOW, you have to claim your power in God's love." She was right. As a COGPOW, my thinking could change, and new possibilities could emerge. In between the situation (A), my feelings (C), and my actions I, I could stop and think (B) and (D). The words of Romans 12:2 kept coming to me: "Wes, 'be transformed by the renewing of your mind'" (NRSV).

I identified the fruit of this transformation as an ability to listen to Becky, to speak slowly, and to consider my words before I said them out loud. Sometimes, Becky needed to express some complex emotions and feelings, and I needed to listen without reacting. So, to live to please the heart of God when I went home, I began to imagine that God was there watching me and cheering me on to maturity. I reminded myself that I was loved and forgiven by God, and I made it my goal to live in that freedom.

Even with these new insights, I often wanted to talk with Bonnie about my latest quarrel with Becky. I secretly wanted Bonnie to take sides, mainly mine! Instead, Bonnie kept asking me the question: "Wes, what can you do to please the heart of God?" As we peeked behind what was fueling my anger, we uncovered three, strong, God-honoring longings of my heart for my relationship with Becky:

First, I longed to talk with Becky about the confusion we were experiencing. If we only could communicate again, we could understand each other and the heartbreaks we were facing. For example, when she cried over her empty arms, I felt the grief as well. We could help each other if I could drop my defenses and anger long enough to cry with her.

Second, I wanted Becky to know that even my failed efforts were out of a deep commitment to her. I wrote this prayer one day, "God, I want so much for Becky to know I love her."

Third, underneath my fear and anger was a desire to have my partner, teammate, and first neighbor back. Becky and I had been steadfast friends for nearly twelve years, and I honestly missed her. Despite my pain-induced immaturity and anger, I was confident she missed me.

This potential was not enough to rescue us. Only God could do that. For my marriage to heal, I needed to put God first in my life. To help me grasp what this was like, Bonnie told me stories of her husband, Ron, a former seminary professor of mine and a man I had always admired. She shared with me about times she experienced difficulties. Ron comforted her without trying to fix her. She offered to me the idea that living to please the heart of God in my house involved primarily my *being* and not my *doing*. Becky needed a friend, a friend who would not react in anger or fear. She needed a "brother in Christ," not an adversary. The more I reordered my life with pleasing the heart of God, the better things went. Things slowly started to change in small ways at home. The disagreements lessened just a bit. Each week, Bonnie encouraged me to keep practicing my new skills.

In our meetings, Bonnie and I usually began by reviewing my previous week. The more we talked, the more I discovered patterns of thinking that were causing me to stay in turmoil. Things were certainly improving at home, but I was only scratching the surface of the new life that I sensed was in front of me. Discovering the order of God's love was the start of *thinking* about my thinking. A lot was going on in my head, and some of it was continuing to undercut me.

To help me further understand the patterns of thinking that were present in my mind, Bonnie introduced me to what she called "The Village." By identifying the voices in "The Village," I realized that my seemingly out-of-control emotional reactions and feelings were not "just the way I was" but emerged from a place of both deep woundedness and potential. I needed to learn the order of God's love, and I also needed to know my own thoughts.

The Village: The Voices Beyond the Wall

Bonnie envisioned each person created by God with a blank *wall* on their soul. "The Wall" of our soul is where God desires to write blessings and murals of love, but where others may have instead scribbled graffiti. My graffiti represents the lies that have appeared on my soul's wall. These needed to be erased and replaced with the truth.

One of the lies on the wall of my soul was this: "This is just how I am." I rarely gave my emotions and reactions the attention before God or others that they were demanding. I would have an angry outburst, and I would excuse it by saying: "Well, that's just how I am." That phrase served as a copout for me to continue my current pattern of behavior.

This kind of thinking hurt my relationships with others. It was hard to be married, be a father, a friend, brother, and son with out-of-control insecurity, fear, and anger.

Since I told myself that "this is just the way I am," that this was somehow my destiny or my "thorn in the flesh," I began a quest to learn simply to manage my woundedness. I spent unbelievable amounts of energy with the goal of controlling the symptoms of my brokenness. I sought psychiatric help, accountability groups, and socially appropriate outlets for my emotional underworld.

The truth was that I was struggling with anger over the loss of our son and a host of other soul-crushing events in life. In my anger, I started punching holes in the walls of our new home. This was not only painful, but costly. I decided a better *sin-management* strategy would be to buy a punching bag. One day when money was tight, I spent hundreds of dollars on a punching bag, boxing gloves, and an apparatus to install it in the garage.

When my wife and I would have a disagreement, I would go to the garage. The only problem was that this strategy only further upset Becky, and while the adrenaline rush alleviated my pain, it would return because nothing was ever resolved.

When it came to anger, I never wanted to stop and ask: "Why am I angry?" Instead, my wall of graffiti gave me this message: "Wes, you are just an angry person."

While on some level that was true at that moment, it hardly meant that I was destined to be an angry person for all time.

My new discovery of an identity as a COGPOW meant that I had new hope. I reasoned that COGPOWs don't need to stay angry their whole lives. Jesus is a savior and wants to save me "to the uttermost" (Heb 7:25 KJV). For me, this meant discovering more about myself. The process Bonnie used to help me overcome my lack of self-awareness was an exercise she called identifying *who* and *what voices* were in my "Village."

Bonnie humorously likened these voices in my village to a gathering of "Smurfs." *The Smurfs* is a Dutch cartoon that found popularity in the United States as a television and movie series. Each episode focuses on a group of small, blue creatures with distinctive white hats who boldly engage in adventures in their forest, often escaping and outwitting their arch enemy Gargamel.

Each Smurf has a distinctive name consisting of an adjective that describes their character, many times followed by *Smurf*. For example, the lead character is Papa Smurf who serves as the wise leader of the colony. Others are named Lazy Smurf, Grouchy Smurf, Brainy Smurf, and even Handy Smurf. You can guess what contributions they each make to the overall village life.

In one appointment, Bonnie asked if I could begin to identify the various Smurfs that made up *Wes Village*. This, at first seemingly silly, exercise disarmed me long enough to cause me to slow down and search my soul for the first time in a very long time.

As I listened to the various voices in my head, I envisioned a group of Smurfs sitting around a campfire for a discussion or a decision, and I took *roll* to see who was there. In the weeks that followed, I began to give them names. The loudest voices insisted going first, of course, so I started with Angry Smurf.

Soon, I had identified about a dozen other Smurfs. There was Rescue Smurf, who liked to come to the rescue of others. There was Strategy Smurf, who liked to have a plan. There was Caring Smurf, who genuinely cared for others. Also sitting around the fire was Laughter Smurf, who had fun and a good sense of humor. Record Keeper Smurf kept a close tally on people around me but even more meticulous records about myself. Creative Smurf liked to find new paths. Scared Smurf was there, sitting next to Sad Smurf, who grieved a lot but I didn't want to ask why. Catastrophe Smurf was there, always waiting for the other shoe to drop. His friend, Anxious Smurf often was nearby as well. There was The *Called* Smurf, who believed God really had a plan for his life, Loving Smurf, who wanted to love like Jesus does, and Chill Smurf, who liked to relax in trusting God.

One Smurf I didn't discover till later, probably because he lurked deep in my soul, was Abandoned Smurf, who was always afraid of being left alone. He liked to hang around with a very mean and elusive Smurf, a fellow I named Unloved Smurf because he liked to say I was unlovable and unworthy of love.

I was amazed at all these characters present in my head and the power they held over me. I soon discovered that, in virtually every decision I made during a day, the Village was present. If I can mix Television show metaphors, these Smurfs formed a Tribal Council like you may have seen on the long-running show *Survivor*. They met often for decisions. Instead of a vote, however, my Village usually let the loudest voice *win* the day.

This gave me welcomed insight because I realized that, when it came to my anger, for example, I was letting one Smurf rule the Village. When I encountered a problem, the whole Tribal Council of Smurfs met, and Anger Smurf howled the loudest and bullied everyone else into submission. If he couldn't do that alone, he would team up with Anxiety Smurf, and they would present me one option in the Tribal Council meeting: "Wes, it's fight or flight time! You'd better fight or run away!" It was no wonder this was my pattern in handling conflict.

This problem was much deeper than the graffiti on my wall. This exercise helped me begin to realize how I was not *just* an angry person, but that my anger was a symptom of far more complexity. If the anger originated in the Village, then change was possible through "The Rules of the Village." These are gifts of God for every COGPOW.

As I returned to Bonnie's office to share my list and insights, Bonnie gave me these Rules of the Village:

Rules of The Village

First, she said, you are a COGPOW, so you rule over the village, not the other way around. You are the king or queen of your village.

This was an empowering role. I suddenly felt hope. Anger Smurf was not going to run portions of my life anymore. I was! I am, after all, to quote Henry Cloud, "Ridiculously in charge" of my actions, emotions, and reactions.[7] A child has no control

---

7   Henry Cloud, *Boundaries for Leaders: Results, Relationships, and Being Ridiculously in Charge* (New York: HarperCollins Publishers, 2013).

over the village. He or she simply does what the village says. Adults, however, are given authority over our own souls.

It was going to take time, but that day, I felt a new beginning as a COGPOW, and I caught at least the vision of a new, mature life.

Second, it is important to "listen in" on what the villagers are saying to each other and to you.

My village was in constant conversation throughout the day. When I recognized this, I was able to trace my behaviors back to these various characters in my head. Suddenly, I was no longer being ambushed by feelings of anger or anxiety in the same way as I had been. As I went through my day, I began to be self-aware of the activity and conversations that were taking place in my mind. Frankly, I discovered that the Village never shuts up!

This alone brought great relief. Instead of missing the important (what I call) Tribal Council meetings, I decided to attend them, to listen to each voice, and ultimately to rule. No wonder I felt ambushed by my own reactions and feelings. I had "missed the meetings" in my mind and fell victim to certain voices in my own anarchist village. They ran around like a dog with no leash. It was chaos! It was going to take a while to get this village in order, but at last, I had hope.

This was not "just the way I am." It was the way it was, but it was getting ready to change. I was going to change it.

Third, any Smurf that does not encourage and value the king or queen (You!) the same way that God does, must either leave the village or be willing to be retrained.

This was, again, an empowering rule. When it came to the renewing of my mind, God and I were not out to build a democracy but a kingdom where, under God's direction, I was in charge of my own life, emotions, thoughts, and behaviors. Just as Jesus cleared the temple of the things that were not of God, I could ask God to help me clear the temple where "the Holy Spirit lives," my own body and soul!

In addition to sitting in on meetings, listening to voices, and ruling the meeting, I took further action. I immediately began to quiet Angry Smurf. He and Anxiety Smurf were going to be a challenge that would honestly take years. In their place, I gave more time to Loving Smurf and his fun friend, Chill Smurf. When they spoke up, it at least balanced the negative voices. Called Smurf got more airtime as well in front of the village.

One day, over three years into meeting with Bonnie, Called Smurf got to make a presentation to the whole village at a Tribal Council meeting. With the support of Caring Smurf, Chill Smurf, and others, we made the decision (along with my wife Becky of course) to move from Kentucky to Florida for an expanded ministry opportunity. When Scared Smurf and Anxious Smurf protested the decision, I told them (since I rule!) that "The Tribe has spoken!" and to go and pack their things.

Over the years since I met with Bonnie, in further counseling, spiritual direction, reading, and prayer, I've discovered that behind each *Smurf* lies a deeper story that is worth exploring.

In my life, Rescue Smurf is a familiar presence. In addition to being a pastor, my father served in volunteer fire departments, flood response units, and as a chaplain in hospitals. My brother and I grew up playing with Dad on real fire trucks and ambulances. It is no wonder, it seems to me, that I became a pastor and a chaplain for a fire department, and my brother became a distinguished emergency room physician as well as FEMA first responder. It's in our family village. If you are in any kind of trouble, the best person to call in the world is my brother. He has a gift of knowing what to do in the most difficult moments of life. For me, having Rescue Smurf in my village is a gift. But he needs coaching and leadership for when I need him and when I don't. This Smurf is good in emergencies, but he's not meant to be *rescuing* in every aspect of my life.

Some Smurfs needed to be exiled from the Village. I happen to be a person who believes in the reality of the devil. He was real for Jesus, and I believe he has been real for me as well. Instead of a cartoon character with a pitchfork, however, the devil (according to Jesus) is the "father of lies" (John 8:44). I found one Smurf who fit this description, and he needed to be exiled.

Unlovable Smurf was the culprit. When I began to embrace the gift of being a Child of God Person of Worth, the voice that said that I was unlovable simply could not co-exist with Jesus in my life. I went to him one day in my prayers, and, with Jesus' backup, I gave him the news: "Unlovable Smurf, the Tribe has spoken, and I have made my decision," I told him. "You've got to go." He's tried occasionally to sneak back in from time to time, but he's basically been gone ever since.

Some Smurfs needed to be retrained. Since they each have a story, I have discovered that the best way to begin this retraining is find out their story, but with great gentleness and love. As Michelangelo used his chisel like a brush, and as Bonnie used her words as a gift, we are to be gentle with ourselves and especially with our woundedness.

The Smurf that took the longest to be healed in my Village was Abandonment Smurf. I grew up in a home with a lot of anxiety. My greatest fear was that my parents would get divorced and leave me alone. While that never happened, the frequent arguments and conflict in our home gave me cause for concern during my formative years. Later, my parents thankfully reconciled and ended up enjoying a beautiful marriage; to their credit, they asked for and received my forgiveness.

However, even though I forgave them, I took that wound that many children experience, and I only made it worse. Instead of offering it to God for healing, I let it remain an open and often infected wound for many years.

A few years ago, I read a book by Brennan Manning called *Abba's Child*. It reinforces my journey, and I commend it to you.[8] In that book, suggested by my most recent counselor, there is a scene in which Brennan has a conversation with an internal voice he calls his "Imposter," a similar personification to the Smurfs that Bonnie introduced to me. What amazed me about Brennan's conversation with this part of himself was the kindness that he had for his Imposter. Instead of angrily silencing his Imposter or kicking him out, Brennan began with this:

> I come to you today not with rod in hand but with an olive branch. When I was a little boy and first knew that no one was there for me, you intervened

---

8   See Brennan Manning, *Abba's Child: The Cry of the Heart for Intimate Belonging* (Colorado Springs, CO: NavPress, 2015).

and showed me where to hide. (In those Depression days of the thirties, you recall, my parents were doing the best they could with what they had just to provide food and shelter.) At that moment in time, you were invaluable. Without your intervention, I would have been overwhelmed by dread and paralyzed by fear. You were there for me and played a crucial, protective role in my development. Thank you.[9]

With my counselor's help, I had a similar meeting with Abandonment Smurf. I began with gratitude that he had been there to give voice to my fears. In addition, Abandonment Smurf's presence propelled me into a friendship with Jesus, even at an early age.

I then gave Abandonment Smurf the news: "I don't need you anymore. I'm an adult now, and I'm choosing to rely on Jesus' promise that he will never leave me 'as an orphan,' that if I 'abide in him,' he promises to 'abide in me'" (see John 15). Abandonment Smurf agreed to go. I wept when I told him the news. He had been a part of me so long that it was hard to let him go.

At the risk of sounding even more strange, I'll tell you that I let Abandonment Smurf stick around in the village but with some retraining and a new assignment. He is to be on the lookout for others who may have fallen victim to the same lie. He's available for me to have compassion for anyone who fears being rejected or left alone. But as a COGPOW, I reclaimed a promise from God who says, "Never will I leave you; never will I forsake you" (Heb 13:5 NIV).

---

9   Manning, 28.

Seven months after I began meeting with Bonnie and began calling myself a COGPOW, I wrote this prayer in my journal. It was a beacon of hope after pages and pages of pleading
for help.

June 3, 2003

Dear Jesus, my Savior, and my Friend,

I am so glad to be with you. Or should I say, WE
are glad to be with you. All of us are here, the whole
gang . . . all my Smurfs! And you! A new growth curve
has begun. I am claiming my adultness, independent
from all identities except my identity in you. It's about
time. Finally. I have been transformed as of late. I am
yours. Child of God. Yes, that's it. I'm not anybody
else. Nothing else matters. I have preached this and
told this to thousands of people but never myself. Wes
is a new creation. My anxiety over what everyone else
thinks of me is slightly fading away. We are all COG-
POWs. I want to be yours. Nothing and no one else.
I am Wes, your son. Up until now I missed it. But all
the while you've been with me. You are doing this good
thing in me. Thank you for your grace.

CHAPTER THREE:
MOONFLOWERS

Spirit of the living God, fall afresh on me.

Melt me, Mold me . . .

A few years ago, my mom Sandy flew down from Kentucky to Florida for a visit. We had a great week together. When I dropped her off at the airport for her flight home, she gave me a goodbye hug and then said with a mischievous smile, "I left some things in your home office for you this morning. Do with them whatever you think is best. Love you, bye!" Before I could say or ask anything, she turned to make her way to her flight.

All day at work, I wondered what she had left for me in my office at home. I had noticed that my mom had an extra suitcase on this visit and assumed she just wanted options for clothes or something. When I got home from church later that day, I ran curiously into my office and burst into laughter at what was waiting for me.

Propped up on my desk was one of the first toys I had as a child, a toy farm that was my absolute favorite. When I was a little kid, I would go into my parents' room, wake them up at 3:00 a.m., and say, "Mommy, Daddy, let's play farm!" Only a parent's love could propel them to wake up with me for play-time in the middle of the night!

For about thirty years, my mom had been asking me to come get my childhood toys out of her house. Before dropping them off with me in Florida, she had moved them at least four times from city to city. I guess she had finally had enough. When I sent her a text *thanking* her for the gifts, she gently reminded me that I'm an adult, and if I want to keep old toys around, I can store them myself.

Suddenly, I had a new problem. My wife got home from work and said to me, "Why do we suddenly have your old toys lying around!" I'll bet my mom knew that would happen!

Now, let me pause here for a moment and admit some-thing to you. I'm aware of what you're probably thinking, "*This ain't right!*" You're correct. It is a bit weird, isn't it? After five decades of life, my mom was telling me, "It's time to pick up and pack up" your toys!

Time to Grow Up

As my visits in Bonnie's office stretched into the end of a second and start of a third year, we slowly turned our attention to the lingering immaturities that were making me miserable. To live the life God had for me meant leaving my old *toys* be-hind. As I began to live to please the heart of God, the Holy

Spirit began to reveal to me more and more the need for me to leave behind my immature thoughts, words, and actions. God had a better way for me to live, and I knew it. I had written papers and preached sermons on maturing in faith. It was time for me to live it!

This was no longer a to-do list of things I had to accomplish to make God love me. Instead, I began to yearn for God to do in me what I could not do for myself. For the first time, I began to understand what Paul wrote about in Ephesians 4. Writing from a prison cell after being arrested for his faith in Jesus, he said this:

> Therefore I, a prisoner for serving the Lord, beg you to lead a life worthy of your calling, for you have been called by God. Always be humble and gentle. Be patient with each other, making allowance for each other's faults because of your love. Make every effort to keep yourselves united in the Spirit, binding yourselves together with peace. (Eph. 4:1-3)

I had embraced the idea of being a COGPOW. Instead of constantly bullying myself, I had a new desire to live into that identity. COGPOW had become my identity and my calling. But I lacked the character to run with my new calling. I lacked the self-discipline and will to get there on my own. I had tried and failed many times. Bonnie invited me to begin to think of myself like clay on a potter's wheel, waiting to be shaped. I could envision this metaphor. Where I grew up, my neighbor was an artist and had a pottery workshop, complete with a wheel and kiln. I would often visit and sit mesmerized, watching her work with a blob of clay, as she would transform it into a beautiful piece of pottery.

Applying this idea to my soul was far less burdensome than my long lists of spiritual *to-do's* that needed to be done so God would love me. Living this new concept for me was as simple as taking time each day to rest in God's love, rather than attempting to do more things for God. The more I regarded myself as a COGPOW, the more I realized that God wanted to mold me more and more into the masterpiece God had in mind. I needed to position my life so that God could do God's work in me, not my work for God.

By getting to know myself through identifying who was in my village, I had a new and growing self-awareness. It was growing more obvious to me that much of my behavior had been a coping mechanism to deal with the unresolved pain in my village. Buying a punching bag was one example of how I attempted to cope with my anger. When I bought it, it was merely for damage control, not healing. Bonnie helped me understand that there was so much more to COGPOW than just a self-affirmation or positive thought. God makes power available for Children of God to experience real change!

Bonnie explained it this way: As a COGPOW, I received a package gift. Since I was a Child of God, that also meant that I was a Person of Worth. I am a COG *and* a POW. They go together. God gives me not only this gift of identity. God also gives me the power to *live into that identity.*

The theme of growing up to live into our new identity permeates the Bible. Paul says that, as we live into our new identity, we can experience the very "fullness of Christ" (Eph. 4:13 NIV), meaning enjoying the same nature and spirit he enjoyed. Living to please the heart of God made me more spiritually aware of my life and the potential of discipleship to move from "one degree of glory to another" (2 Cor 3:18 ESV). This possibility awakened me anew to the Holy Spirit's power. I began to have new hope that the same life Jesus experienced could also be mine. This is what I read Paul saying in his letter to the Ephesians:

> Then we will no longer be immature like children. We won't be tossed and blown about by every wind of new teaching. We will not be influenced when people try to trick us with lies so clever, they sound like the truth. Instead, we will speak the truth in love, growing in every way more and more like Christ, who is the head of his body, the church. (Eph. 4:14-15)

Paul gave me a vision of what it looks like to be *grown up* in my faith. I don't need to stay immature, susceptible to the opinions or words of others or to lies that I tell myself. That sounded like a wonderful way to live, but I was so far from it that it seemed like a distant dream. I tried disqualifying myself from the start: "*This could never be me*," I thought.

The real challenge for me was accepting that living into this new maturity would involve significant change on my part. Living like Christ was not me! When Bonnie and I began to explore this topic, I said to her, "Okay, but Bonnie, change is hard work! I don't change so easily. I fail at it over and over again." Immediately, she challenged my conviction on the topic of change. "When you approach it that way," she explained, "then you are setting yourself up for failure." She reassured me that I was not alone in my reaction to the idea of change.

"There was a cartoon I saw once," she began, "with this caption: 'Change is good as long as I don't have to do anything differently.' Wes, lots of people have trouble with change, but I want to help you understand this in a new way." Change, Bonnie explained, is part of God's design for us. Change is how God takes us from an old place to a new place in life. That year, we began a journey together to understand how God brings change.

God's ways are different from our ways when it comes to transformation and change. I always viewed change as something I had to do apart from God. The truth is that I can't do much for very long relying only on my own resources. I needed God to do what I could not. I soon discovered that God had given me both the gift of an identity and the *power* to live into that identity.

The type of change Bonnie was speaking about did not involve "pulling myself up" or "getting it together." She said, "Wes, all power in heaven and earth has been given to Jesus, who wants to give maturity to you as God's child. But just because you have it doesn't mean you are using it. Don't abuse yourself by saying you are unable to change and look for situations that support that. Remember the rule: You do not abuse a child of God."

At the same time, Bonnie explained that I do not need to insult God by saying I cannot change. She encouraged me to speak possibilities into my own life. Things like,

- I rule my village!

- God gives me the power to change!

- Because God is with me, I can claim God's power at any time in any situation to think, feel, and act in loving, joyful, and peaceful ways.

- God is for me not against me.

These were new *absolutes* for the wall of my soul. Each involved me taking the power that God had granted to me to be, as Bonnie described it, "an adult and to put away childish ways." Just as Jesus grew in wisdom and stature (Luke 2:52), I could too!

Putting Away Childish Ways

In the movie, *Toy Story 3*, the little boy named Andy from the first movie has now become an adult and is preparing to go to college. As a part of this transition, Andy's mom gives him a garbage bag and asks him to sort through the old toys he wanted her to hold onto and those to give away. Since these toys talk, this was the backdrop for an exciting adventure.

As a newly named COGPOW, I soon discovered that "putting away my toys and growing up" was far more than a self-affirmation or a mantra to feel good. An identity as God's child came with the power to establish real, lasting change. I found that the real adventure of living as a COGPOW would begin when I took an inventory of my life, my Wall, and my Village and was willing to put away old ways. Only then could God give me something new.

As Bonnie shared this process with me, she pulled out her Bible. She turned to the *love* chapter, 1 Corinthians 13. I often read this chapter on love when I officiated at weddings. Bonnie explained that there is verse in this chapter that most people miss, yet is vital for living into an identity as a COGPOW. Here's what she read: "When I was a child, I spoke and thought and reasoned as a child. But when I grew up, I put away child-ish things" (1 Cor 13:11).

This was a verse that I usually skipped over. I had always thought that statement to be a little out of place compared to the rest of the chapter. The other parts about love being "patient and kind" and "not conceited or boastful or proud" were more poetic and understandable. Little did I know that those two sentences would be the key to moving the concept COGPOW from my heart and head into my daily life and core identity.

Paul writes that he used to speak, think, and reason as a child. But when he grew up, he put away childish things. These childish ways included his old ways of talking, the opinions he held, and the way he reasoned about life.

As I had begun to grow in self-awareness through tools like the Wall and my Village, it was clear to me that I had my own set of "childish ways." Like Paul, my list included many of the words I spoke, the thoughts I had, and my often-immature rea-soning. Until this time with Bonnie, my immediate response to this type of honest assessment of my life would have been despair and paralysis. This time, however, something felt differ-ent. Certainly, I felt remorse, but I also had hope. I realized that a new power was available to me (as they say in AA) that could "restore me to sanity."

For perhaps the first time in my life, I read this list in First Corinthians not as a call to "work harder," "do more," "shape up," or as any other *should* or *ought*. I knew those were dead ends. Instead, I heard them as an invitation to be with Jesus more. For the first time, I recognized new things in the story of Jesus that I had missed in my task-heavy approach to self-discipleship. Jesus taught his disciples about attitudes called the *be-attitudes*. Jesus didn't teach amassing to-do lists. In Jesus' final night with his disciples, he didn't shout (as I had done to myself), "Guys, get it together already!" Instead, he said, "Abide in my love" (see John 15). In my new reading of the stories of Jesus, I could imagine Jesus saying to me, "Wes, abide in me, and we will work together to put childish ways behind you, so you can have joy in your life!"

Joy. That had been missing in my life. But with Bonnie's help and with new waves of grace flowing into my life through the Spirit of the Living God, verses about joy began to almost jump off the page. One of my new favorites was when Jesus says, "I have said these things to you so that my joy may be in you, and that your joy may be complete" (John 15:11 NRSV). In my emerging identity as a COGPOW, I could now begin to believe and see that a life of joy was possible for me. Yes, it would involve change. But the change Jesus speaks of is so much less heavy than my self-attempts at finding maturity. Jesus' path is filled with joy. Even his path of change is filled with joy.

With this new approach to change, I opened my life to God in new ways. Together, God and I could put away my old ways like packing up old toys. In their place, I realized that God could not only could give me a new identity as a COGPOW; God had the power to help me live into that identity.

For me, this soul-deep transformation began by asking God in prayer to look with me at what areas of my life needed changing. I recognized again that the change I needed was not going to occur through my hard work but through God's healing power.

A Brave Prayer

Praying and talking with God daily was crucial to claiming and resting in my COGPOW. During this time, I found I loved simply talking and being with God. In Psalm 139, I found a model prayer to help me. I had heard the stories of the Old Testament hero David since I was a child. I have vivid memories of my mom or dad reading me stories about David fighting Goliath or hiding from his enemy, King Saul. Now, as a newly self-aware adult, it was how David handled his flaws that captured my attention. I liked that David was a flawed hero of faith. Even though our circumstances were vastly different, I imagined that he must have struggled to know his own identity as a COGPOW. I admired how, in his failures, he kept coming back to God. Maybe that tenacity alone is why he was described in Scripture as "a man after God's own heart" (1 Sam 13:14). I resolved to be like David in that I would keep coming back to God no matter what, throwing myself at God's feet with raw honesty.

In one of David's prayers, I found words that expressed the state of my own soul and my desire to be transformed. I was desperate for a new life that I could not experience with my own strength, so the way David invited God into his anxiety became my mantra. I even memorized these two verses:

Search me, O God, and know my heart;

   test me and know my anxious thoughts.

Point out anything in me that offends you

   and lead me along the path of everlasting life.

(Ps 139:23-24)

What I liked about this prayer was that I could honestly invite God into my soul. For me, it was as if I were saying to God, "I've been looking at the wall of my soul and the village of voices inside of my head. We have concluded that we need help!" It also seemed to me that this was a somewhat dangerous prayer. I had done a lot of praying in my life, especially at times during my health crisis and Daniel's death, but never with the honesty and self-awareness I was offering to God now. I used David's words to invite God to shine the light of God's love into the darkest places in my soul.

As I looked at the words of those two verses from David's prayer, I saw that the process of change for David involved God first searching and knowing him, then naming what needed to be changed, and then God leading that change. I began asking God to search and know me in three ways.

First, I needed God to help me with the old messages of graffiti on the wall of my soul. Second, I needed God to help me with painful memories that kept resurfacing in my emotions, often in ways that ambushed me. Third, I needed God's help with a new way to deal with my past mistakes, the ones I held onto and frequently used to bully myself. All the work I had done with Bonnie up until this point seemed to have, at last, brought me to a place where I was finally ready to ask God to change my life.

First, I invited God to help me to erase the old messages I had been living by, which blocked me from the "path of everlasting life." Like everyone, I had lots of graffiti on the wall of my soul. Some frankly needed erasing, especially the mantras that I repeated about never being "good enough" and the perceived flaws that left me "unlovable." I never really discovered where these had their beginning and how they made it onto my wall. I have no memory of anyone ever flat out telling me something so horrible. Nonetheless, they were there on my wall and needed to be erased.

Another old message needed erasing too: "I'm just an angry person. That's who I am." So did, "Wes, you are just a failure." And "If you want to be loved, you'd better hide your true self." This one was supported by statements like, "You'd better make others happy!" and "Wes, you are the only one who has this problem." The fear of terminal uniqueness kept me hiding. Somehow, my wall also had these statements scribbled across it: "You are worthless" and "lazy." Through prayer, God gently revealed my list of old messages.

God helped me name and expose old memories too. I had a memory bank of painful experiences and fear that remained so well hidden that I barely was aware of them. Even though the memories themselves remained hidden from me, the emotions surrounding those memories and events remained as alive and real as they were the moment they first occurred. In the safety of prayer, God began to reveal those memories to me.

One of my painful memories involved my father getting angry and leaving our house when I was seven or eight years old. I have no idea what was going on with him at the time, but I knew he was upset, and I heard him say he was leaving. I begged him not to go, even holding on to his leg and begging him to stay. To my despair and despite my pleading, he left. I still have no idea if he was gone a couple of hours or a couple of days, but fear of abandonment took root in me. Memories are often factually unreliable or even untrue; in my childhood mind, however, we never talked about that day or debriefed what was going on when he returned.

This was a memory that was buried deeply in my soul, yet the emotions of anxiety and fear were always present just below the surface, often coming out in moments when, as an adult, I felt like that little boy decades ago, holding on to his daddy's leg. My raw fear was that God would do the same to me if I screwed up: He would leave. The strange thing in this experience of remembering was that, as God revealed this and other painful memories to me, I felt a safety and gentleness present in my soul that hadn't been there before. Bonnie's mantra was ever present: COGPOWs never abuse another COGPOW, especially themselves. The Spirit of the Living God reassured me that, even if I could never forget what happened in those times of pain, I soon could remember those times in a brand new way.

Feeling safer, I invited God to join me in looking at my past mistakes. I had a list of actions and attitudes that were a part of my story that I didn't want anyone to know about. I liked to try to keep them hidden from God and myself. I didn't like to think of these failures. I just tried to go along like nothing happened. But I couldn't escape my own thoughts. It seemed that "everywhere I went, there I was!" My mind remained in a constant cycle of *replay*.

I kept replaying over and over again a semester of bad grades in high school. I replayed how I responded in anger to a supervisor at one of my previous jobs. Some mistakes were more recent, and these were fresh in my mind. No matter how irrational it seemed, I still thought that my son's death was in some way my fault. Did I not pray hard enough? My reckless words to Becky made this worse. My leadership mistakes replayed over and over again in my head, as well. Despite trying to abide by the rule that a COGPOW never abuses another COGPOW, the way I spoke to myself when looking at these memories was downright awful. I needed God's help and healing in a profound way.

I had known that Jesus offered people the gift of forgiveness and new life. Yet I had this line of secret graffiti firmly written onto the wall of my soul: "I can forgive others, but I will never forgive myself!" At last, as I prayed for God to join me in searching my soul, a brand new experience of love and forgiveness came into my life. None of my old messages, memories, or mistakes were easy to talk about with either Bonnie or God, but the more I did, the more something amazing and supernatural took place. I found healing. I found salvation. I found forgiveness. I found myself.

The first book Bonnie asked me to read was by Robert McGee. What I was experiencing in prayer during that time I found in McGee's book:

> We must give up our own efforts to achieve righteousness and instead believe that Christ's death and resurrection alone are sufficient to pay for our sin and separation from God.[10]

---

10   Robert S. McGee, *The Search for Significance: Seeing Your True Worth through God's Eyes* (Nashville, TN: Thomas Nelson, 2003), 16.

Jesus took the graffiti that was on my wall and began to erase it! I began to feel something that I had occasionally encountered before, but never for long: I felt free! Through prayer, naming the graffiti on my wall, and my helplessness to change, I found that Jesus' death and resurrection were enough for me. I was being rescued.

The strange thing about the way God began to bring transformation into my life was that God used the absolute worst of me to give me the best of God. I had spent so much time and energy hiding the parts of myself I considered unlovable. Yet I discovered that the more I invited Jesus into those dark places of my soul, the more love I experienced from God. What a strange tradeoff! It doesn't really add up, but it is real. The more I told God about my old messages, memories, and mistakes, the more love I experienced from God. God never left me. I never sensed God speaking harshly to me or shaming me. God was gentle and kind. It was God's kindness that led to my redemption.

Out of that pain, something new, something good, something of God started emerging in me. God began to turn my mourning into dancing. God began to lift my sorrows.

Have you ever heard of a moonflower? My mom loves to garden, and she introduced me to these amazing plants that she has growing near her front door. They have heart-shaped leaves, tear-shaped bulbs, and a sweet scent.

What is amazing about these flowers is that they only bloom at night. When you walk by them in the sunlight, they are quite ordinary. But at night, they bloom with beautiful white flowers, which is why some gardeners call them "common night glory" flowers. Others call them "Angel's Trumpet!" When I saw these for the first time a few weeks ago, I immediately thought of them as a picture of God's love present with me in my darkest messages, memories, and mistakes. God is at work in my life, even in the times of my life that were shaped by darkness and tears. I wrote in my journal, "Sometimes God's work in my life only emerges in the darkest nights of my soul."

God didn't cause the pain I liked to keep hidden in the dark, but God could redeem that pain and make something beautiful from it. There's an old hymn chorus that begins "Something beautiful, something good." It ends like this:

> All I had to offer Him was brokenness and strife
>
> But he made something beautiful of my life.[11]

In those days, I began *living* the story of the moonflower: The light of God's love was being revealed in the darkest places of my soul. These exercises in ruthless honesty before God, Bonnie, and myself gave me new insight and perspective on my pain. The more I invited God into my darkness, the less scary to me the thought of change and maturity all became.

Growing Young

Not only was my fear lessened, so was my burden. I had heard and even preached the invitation of Jesus, "my yoke is easy . . . and the burden . . . light" (Matt 11:30), but now I began to actually *experience* it. When I was championing my own need for change, I filled my mind with dozens of self-improve-

---

11 William J. and Gloria Gaither, "Something Beautiful," © 1971 William J. Gaither, Inc.

ment goals and deadlines to accomplish them. But as I decided to rest in God's grace and let God do for me what I could not do on my own, I found a lightness in my being. I reframed my ideas of needing to *grow up* to what I sensed in God's invitation to me. God was inviting me to *grow young*.

God and I began to partner together in putting away my childish ways with a joy-laden (not guilt-laden) approach. As I stepped into the new freedom that God had blessed me with by beginning to erase old graffiti, I sensed that God was inviting me to be more childlike. There is a difference in being *childish* and *childlike*. The dictionary defines *childish* as having "immaturity and lack of poise" while *childlike* is "marked by innocence, trust, and simplicity."[12] Wow, what a difference. I liked that God invited me to simplicity, not more complexity. God wanted to restore and return the innocence that I had as a boy, staring in wonder at the stars as well as marveling at the story of Jesus and his love. God desired to give me childlike trust in God again.

All these thoughts were confirmed in me through Jesus' teaching. Jesus instructs his disciples that to mature in faith in God is to become more childlike. Instead of immature self-reliance, I was invited to grow in my reliance on God. This is what I think Jesus was teaching in Matthew 18:1-4:

> About that time the disciples came to Jesus and asked, "Who is greatest in the Kingdom of Heaven?"
>
> Jesus called a little child to him and put the child among them. Then he said, "I tell you the truth, unless you turn from your sins and become like little children,

---

12 "Childish" and "Childlike," *Merriam-Webster.com Dictionary*, Merriam-Webster, https://www.merriam-webster.com/dictionary/childish. Accessed 13 Oct. 2022.

you will never get into the Kingdom of Heaven. So anyone who becomes as humble as this little child is the greatest in the Kingdom of Heaven."

Jesus invites me and his other followers to grow young. Jesus describes becoming childlike as becoming "humble." In Greek, this word means "to make low." By letting Jesus be my leader, I am receptive and responsive to his direction.

As I study the life of Jesus, this is part of the simplicity that Jesus had in his daily life. Jesus' goal was just to do what the Father told him to do and speak what the Father told him to say (John 10:37; 12:50). I had made discipleship heavy and so complex. Jesus kept it as simple as a game of "Follow the Leader." As Jesus followed the lead of his Father, Jesus invites me to follow him.

The paradox of spiritual growth lies in Jesus' invitation for us to trust in him. To live into my God-given identity, to mature in faith, was to become childlike in my trust and reliance upon Jesus.

When I chose to trust God to do in me what I could not do for myself, I found the secret to transformation. Through the power of the Holy Spirit, God continues to do this work in me, as I position my life to follow him.

For a long season of my Christian life, I viewed "becoming like Jesus" as code for me to "try harder." I would speak harshly to myself with such encouraging words such as "Stop it Wes!" or "Hurry up and become more patient!" "Stop thinking bad things" or "You shouldn't be so selfish." I viewed prayer and reading the Bible as a divinely endorsed self-improvement plan in which I had to white-knuckle my own maturity. I was going to get my sanctification the old-fashioned way. I was going to earn it!

In my exhaustion, I not only found encouragement from Bonnie and in my times in prayer, but I also found a friend through the writings of Henri Nouwen. In his books, he described his own struggle with praying, serving others, avoiding temptation, and reading the Bible. He said he failed over and over again, to the point that he began to despair in his efforts to "find God":

> Now I wonder whether I have sufficiently realized that during all this time God has been trying to find me, to know me, and to love me. The question is not "How am I to find God?" but "How am I to let myself be found by him?" The question is not "How am I to know God?" but "How am I to let myself be known by God?" And, finally, the question is not "How am I to love God?" but "How am I to let myself be loved by God?" God is looking into the distance for me, trying to find me, and longing to bring me home.[13]

Instead of my own exhausting religious performance, what I was really needing was God's supernatural presence. The words of Bill Thrall came to my mind: "God doesn't want my excellence; God wants my humility so that he can reflect his excellence."[14]

13　Henri Nouwen, "Meditation 259: Henry Nouwen: God Longs to Bring Me Home," *The Spirit of Life: A Catholic Community of Justice and Joy,* accessed September 23, 2022, https://www.spiritoflifecommunity.org/liturgy/pastors-letter/355-meditation-259-henri-nouwen-god-longs-to-bring-me-home-1-21-2021. See also Henri Nouwen, *The Return of the Prodigal Son: A Story of Homecoming* (New York, NY: Doubleday, 1994).

14　This statement was made by Bill Thrall at Leadership Network on 2/27/2008 in Dallas, Texas.

Bonnie explained to me that COGPOWs who live into their privilege and the freedom of grace simply create opportunities in their days and weeks to encounter Jesus. "God cannot get in to change anything in me without my permission," Bonnie said. For me, this meant laying down my plans for self-improvement and control so that I could give God space in my day.

As a COGPOW, I now made myself available, so God could pour more love into my life. This type of growth involved only my cooperation and involvement. In practical terms, this meant:

- If I wanted to read the Bible in the morning, I needed to go to bed earlier.

- If I wanted a Christian community to walk alongside me, I needed to make time and be available to meet with other friends.

- If I struggled with an addiction or an affliction, I needed to choose recovery and humble myself to get help.

- If I wanted to grow into an awareness of God's presence in my daily life, I needed to slow down and turn off my electronics.

I needed to let go of "childish ways." I began to ask God for help to put away immature thinking patterns, mantras, beliefs, and behaviors, so that I could take up childlike trust.

This forever changed the way I approached change. I used to start lists of improvements. Now, I asked God to show me what I needed to let go of, so that my hands could be open for more of what God had for me.

This change in thinking was confirmed again through reading my Bible. With my new eyes as a COGPOW, I saw for the first time that when Jesus called people, he didn't pile on to-do lists. Instead, Jesus helped people to see what they needed let go of and how to leave some things behind:

- Peter let go of his nets.

- The woman at the well left behind her water jar.

- Levi left behind his tax collector's booth.

- Mary, Martha's sister, let go of her chores to sit at Jesus' feet.

- Lazarus left his grave.

One story that captured my imagination was the story of Jesus' encounter with a rich young ruler in Mark's Gospel. This man came to Jesus, fell on his knees, and asked a genuine question: "What must I do to inherit eternal life?" They talked about the commandments, and the man assured Jesus that he had followed them since he was a boy. Then Mark inserted a fascinating detail into the story: "*Jesus looked at him and loved him*" (Mark 10:17-21 NIV, italics added). There's that COGPOW gift again! Jesus looked at him and *loved* him. Tears welled up in my eyes as I read this in my newly accepted identity as a COGPOW. Then, out of love, Jesus said to the man that he needed to go and "sell everything" he had, "give it to the poor," and come and follow Jesus.

Before this time in my life, I always viewed this encounter with a harshness that was my own interpretation, not Mark's. I assumed that Jesus was giving this man a list of *to-do's*, like I did for myself. The to-do items seemed extreme. I imagined Jesus saying with an authoritative tone, "Go sell everything! Then you will be qualified."

Now, I suddenly read this encounter through a whole new lens. Jesus started with love for this man. Then, with love, he helped the man let go of something that was a burden for him, so he could be free to follow Jesus. For me, it was not an over-abundance of possessions that I needed to let go of, it was a plethora of self-criticism and attempts at self-righteousness. Jesus' loving invitation to the rich young ruler and to me were to "let go," so he could give us something new, his love and life! Perhaps this is what it meant when Jesus said, "whoever wants to save their life will lose it, but whoever loses their life for me will find it" (Matt 16:25 NRSV). When I was ready to let go, then I could receive soul-deep transformation.

I can tell you this. If you find that you are serious about embarking on this journey of putting away childish ways, my personal experience and my nearly thirty years of pastoral ministry have led me to believe that this is not work that can be done alone. I encourage you to begin to pray about seeking out a counselor, a trusted friend or friends, a recovery group such as Al-Anon or Alcoholics Anonymous, a spiritual director, or some other person(s) to join you in this journey of transformation. COGPOWs need other COGPOWs to encourage them along their journey of change.

For a season, Bonnie and a trusted group of friends served me in that way. It was through their prayers, examples, presence, and encouragement that I was able to position my life in a way that the Spirit of the Lord could free me from one unrelenting Smurf: Angry Smurf.

Angry Smurf Finds Healing

Angry Smurf and I have a long history together. When I was a child and teenager, I was a handful when I got mad, especially for my mom and dad. Bonnie knew me well then and can testify to my destructive temper fueled by huge amounts of fear and anxiety.

This problem with anger continued through my twenties and into my early thirties. For many years, I had tried to *manage* this sin. I told myself and others, "I'm terrible at conflict. This is just the way I am."

Over time, however, as Bonnie and I took the roll of who was present in my Village, and God began to erase some of the graffiti on my Wall, I sensed that change might be possible for me in this area.

As I positioned my life before the Spirit of the Lord through more times of prayer and with the help of several people who were filled with both grace and truth, I learned that anger was a secondary emotion. For me, anger came from trying to make other people happy, so that I would feel loved and accepted. My anger emerged from my own fear of abandonment. At its core, my anger was an identity issue. I still wasn't quite living into my COGPOW-ness.

My first move had been to take my need to God. At this point, I knew many of my childish ways. The problem was that I was paralyzed by them and had accepted "the way I was" as the final word in my life. When I invited Jesus into the darkness of my anger, he helped me see that I had a wound that only he could heal. I sensed in prayer that Jesus offered to love the anger right out of my soul.

With the help and encouragement of others who were praying for me, I began to search out what the Bible said about anger. One day, as I listened to a sermon by Pastor Rick Warren, he shared a verse from James that has become a mantra for my life. James 1:19-20 (NIV) says this about anger: "My dear brothers and sisters, take note of this: Everyone should be quick to listen, slow to speak, and slow to become angry, because human anger does not produce the righteousness that God desires."

Pastor Warren pointed out something simple yet incredible about this instruction from Jesus' half-brother, James. That is, if I am "quick to listen" and "slow to speak," the result is that I'll be "slow to anger."

Instead of praying that everyone around me would stop making me mad, I prayed that God might change me. I prayed this verse thousands of times. "God, help me today to be quick to listen, slow to speak, and slow to become angry."

Over the course of several months, when conflict came into my day and life, I started the new practices found in this verse. I sought first to listen. I listened not only to what the other person was saying but also to myself. I examined my own insecurities and fears that were at work in the conflict. I joined the Village for lots of meetings where I heard the perspectives of each Smurf in my brain.

Then, when I could, I asked for time. This was one way to "slow my speaking." I've found that other people hate conflict so much that if I remain able to listen and then ask for a few minutes, or hours, or even a few days of time, they are glad to give it. Anything is better than another conflict! Over time, this buffer of time began to help me to *respond* instead of *react* in heated moments. The results of being quick to listen and slow to speak did indeed make it easier to be "slow to anger."

Additionally, instead of trying to manage my anger, I began to trust God to heal me and mold me into a new person filled with peace. One night, I took my punching bag out to the curb and threw it away. That old *toy* had to go. It was time to grow up. The next morning, the garbage truck took it away, and I took up a new childlike trust. My wife wept again, but this time with tears of gratitude.

I wasn't instantly cured by any means, but a change began inside of me that is still going on to this day. In those dark places of anger, my Moonflower became an Angel's Trumpet, as I experienced how God can make love bloom even in the dark.

Ten years later, I was in a meeting with a group of people who were at odds with each other. The meeting became heated. As I watched what was going on in the room, my village's Angry Smurf and I (yes, I let him stay) saw lots of people who reminded us of our "old Wes." At the end of the meeting, two people waited to talk to me. They said, "You were so cool and calm with all that anger swirling around and even coming at you. How on earth did you pull that off?" I laughed with joy at the Spirit of the Lord reaching another degree of glory in me. I smiled and replied with gratitude and just said, "It's a very, very long story."

I've discovered that, as God began a new work of molding me into a new creation, I could rest assured that, by grace, I have not only received the gift of new identity as a COGPOW, but I also was given the power to live into this new identity. For every *command to* in the Bible, God gives me the *power to* live that transformation in my life.

The Glory of Being Loved by the Father of Jesus

In chapter 2, I compared God's work in my life to the artist Michelangelo. To create his masterpiece, "David," Michelangelo simply chipped away anything in the marble that was not David.

When we position ourselves in God's hands, God gently and yet firmly molds us into a divinely designed masterpiece. In many ways God chips away at anything in you that is not *you*.

The apostle Paul wrote that we must "put away childish things" (Eph 4). He said that through God's shaping and molding, we reflect the image of God in our individual lives. Through the power of God's Spirit working in and through us, we are "changed from one degree of glory to another" (2 Cor 3:18 ESV).

God's glory is God's infinite honor and worth. While this is a lofty concept, Jesus comes to planet earth in human form to give us a picture of what this glory looks like in everyday life, with all its inglorious twists and turns. John, Jesus' friend and biographer, tells us that we can get a picture of God's glory by looking at Jesus. John refers to Jesus as "The Word" in his account and begins with these words: "So the Word became human and made his home among us. He was full of unfailing love and faithfulness. And we have seen his glory, the glory of the Father's one and only Son" (John 1:14 NLT).

The Glory of God the Father is revealed through Jesus the Son. And by the power of God's Holy Spirit working in us, a metamorphosis takes place and restores us to reflecting the image of God in our lives. This is life as a COGPOW: The damaging graffiti on the wall of your soul is replaced with a beautiful mural of God's goodness and love, uniquely expressed by you! St. Irenaeus is quoted as saying, "The glory of God is a person fully alive." Jesus' words can be a comfort to all: "I came that they may have life and have it abundantly" (John 10:10 NRSV).

Brennan Manning tells the story of Edward Farrell, a priest from Detroit, who went on a two-week summer vacation to Ireland to visit his one living uncle who was about to celebrate his eightieth birthday.

> On the great day, the priest and his uncle got up before dawn.... They took a walk along the shores of Lake Killarney and stopped to watch the sunrise, standing side by side with not a word exchanged.... Suddenly the uncle turned and went skipping down the road. He was radiant, beaming, smiling from ear to ear.
>
> His nephew said, "Uncle Seamus, you really look happy."
>
> "I am, lad."
>
> "Want to tell me why?"
>
> His eighty-year-old uncle replied, "Yes, you see, my Abba [the Father of Jesus] is very fond of me."[15]

---

15   Manning, 46.

This man's life was anchored in God's love for him.

The more I trusted God with the darkness of my own soul, the more I discovered the Father of Jesus is very fond of me, too. In the security of that love, I began to find healing.

CHAPTER FOUR:
QUIET WATERS

Spirit of the living God, fall afresh on me.
Melt me, Mold me, Fill me . . .

About a year before I began meeting with Bonnie, the Board of Ordained Ministry of my denomination required I take part in a unique class entitled *Clinical Pastoral Education* (CPE). This course is the primary way people providing spiritual care in hospital and hospice settings begin their training. I took it simply because it was required for my ordination. The five-month, immersive experience involved both serving as a student chaplain for an in-patient hospice unit as well as taking part in a peer group led by a CPE supervisor. At the hospice unit, under the close watch of a seasoned chaplain, I had the opportunity to serve and support over sixty persons of all ages facing terminal illnesses. I had the honor of being with over a dozen of these patients as they took their last breath.

This experience was a demanding, yet life-changing, training ground for me. The doctors, nurses, chaplains, my peers, and the CPE supervisor taught me the power of simple skills such as listening and the importance of presence. When appropriate, the staff and leaders affirmed my gifts. However, by far the greatest help they gave me were the times they named the brokenness in my life that I was either unaware of (at best) or had tried to conceal from others.

Near the end of the semester, in one of my last one-on-one meetings with my well-credentialed and seasoned CPE supervisor named Carol, I realized she was discovering my struggles with people pleasing, anxiety, insecurity, and exhausting codependency. For about an hour, she began to name these observations that deep down I knew were true. I thought I had been successful in keeping them hidden for nearly four months, but by the last month she was *onto* the real me. So were my peers. My schedule was so packed that I was often late to class or group projects. In my peer review, she revealed that my student-colleagues at hospice nicknamed me, "The Late Wes Olds." Not funny.

In my final report, she then included these poignant warnings that would soon re-surface in my life:

> I am concerned that Wes will sabotage himself through his over-extension and poor boundaries . . . I would encourage him to find an objective, supportive person or group to whom he would be accountable for ongoing growth and development. Otherwise, I'm concerned that he will get so caught up in ministering to others that he neglects his personal, spiritual, and professional growth.

She wasn't done! She continued . . .

I am <u>particularly</u> concerned that if Wes fails to address these [boundary] issues early on that he could easily burn out due to lack of self-care or attention to family life.

The underlined word *particularly* stung, along with the repeated use of the word *concerned*. I was busted. For reasons I did not yet understand, I wanted this weakness of mine to stay hidden.

Only months later, all these warnings proved to be true and were the root cause of my burnout and *crash*. As Bonnie worked with me on claiming my new identity as a Child of God Person of Worth, it became clear that my new life would need to involve new rules and ways and of relating to God, myself, and others.

I needed God's help, not only putting away childish ways and erasing old graffiti; I needed God to write a new mural on the wall of my soul. I needed *continually* to be filled with God's love and love for myself. With the old graffiti erased, I longed for new blessings to fill the reconditioned wall of my soul.

Bonnie explained this stage of my journey this way: "[You have] a new wall on which you and God design the amazing person he had in mind for you from the very beginning!"

That sounded good to me!

Fill Me with Love for God

As you recall, one of Bonnie's anchor verses in counseling that we came back to several times was Jesus' Greatest Commandment. Jesus said that his followers were to "Love the Lord your God with all your heart and with all your soul and with all your mind and with all your strength. The second is this: Love your neighbor as yourself. There is no commandment greater than these" (Mark 12:30-31 NIV).

These words of Jesus helped me to clarify the order of love as loving God, loving self, loving others. They also taught me how we are designed to love God: with all our heart, soul, mind, and strength. Bonnie summarized this teaching by encouraging me freely to love God with all my mind, body, and spirit.

As I got started in this makeover, I remembered the wisdom of Dallas Willard: "Grace is not opposed to effort, grace is opposed to earning."[16] Learning from my experience of healing with anger, which I shared in the last chapter, I began to first create space in my life to love God and let God love me. This was an *all-in* invitation. Like the song, "The Hokey Pokey," I had to put my *whole self in*: mind, body, and spirit!

In the freedom of forgiveness and grace, Bonnie taught me that I love God with my mind by:

- Monitoring what the Village is saying and giving attention to any Smurf that does not honor God.

- Making choices that please the heart of God, and welcoming change by giving new permissions to myself in life.

- Defining my life by my new identity, not old labels.

- Recognizing I have options, for God is able to do more than I could ask or imagine.

---

16   Dallas Willard, *The Great Omission: Reclaiming Jesus's Essential Teachings on Discipleship,* San Francisco, CA: HarperOne, 2014), 34.

I love God with my body by:

- Valuing my body and caring for the temple that God calls home in me.

- Delighting in a life of no shame and enjoying the splendor of God's creation of me.

- Placing my body as an active, connected part of the church, the body of Christ—called in Scripture the *ecclesia*—the called-out and gathered people of God.

I love God with my spirit by:

- Bearing the fruit of "love, joy, peace, patience, kindness, goodness, faithfulness, gentleness, and self-control" while guided by the Holy Spirit (Gal 5:22-25).

- Developing an ever-deepening friendship with God.

- Taking on the attitude of a joyful servant of others and allowing others to serve me.

In beginning to apply these new rules for my own life, I gained a fresh perspective on life and God's love. God's love used to seem like a destination that I could never arrive at because of all my (and others') problems, no matter how hard I tried to solve them. One of the reasons I did not want my CPE supervisor to know my weaknesses was because I thought it somehow meant I had failed to *arrive* at loving God with my mind, body, and spirit.

I soon began to discover that God's love is not a destination. Instead, in my new childlike trust of God, I found that life really is more about the journey with Jesus as my leader.

Henri Nouwen captures this well in his book, *Spiritual Direction*. He says, "Your life, my life, is given graciously by God.

Our lives are not problems to be solved but journeys to be taken with Jesus as our friend and finest guide."[17]

The Beautiful *More-ness* of the Heart of God

My journey of counseling did not end with Bonnie. Far from it. Instead, her love and wisdom opened the possibility that, any time in the coming years that I felt troubled, I could seek the counsel of friends, support groups, and recovery meetings. I could also find healing and freedom through the ministry of mental-health professionals, including psychiatrists, psychologists, and therapists. Until my time with Bonnie, a stigma created in part by my own fear, prevented me from seeking such help.

A few years ago, I had the opportunity to spend two weeks at a counseling and retreat center for pastors called *Quiet Waters*. In addition to the rest and healing this ministry provided, one of the best parts of this experience was traveling and seeing the national parks that surrounded Denver. I had never been to Colorado before, so during my breaks I went to explore the sights.

My favorite place by far was Rocky Mountain National Park. I have always enjoyed mountains, and this place had majestic peaks like I had never seen before!

Since I was by myself, I wanted to make sure to take plenty of selfies that I could bring back and share with my family and friends. As soon as I drove up to the entrance of the park, I stopped the car and found what I considered "the most beautiful spot" I'd ever been to in my life. I had to figure out how to

---

17 Henri Nouwen, *Spiritual Direction: Wisdom for the Long Walk of Faith* (New York, NY: HarperOne, 2006), 6.

prop up my phone, learn to use the timer, and position myself just right, so I could take a selfie. I called my wife Becky to tell her about it.

I got back into the car. I drove a few hundred yards more into the park, I came around a bend and saw guess what? *Here* was "the most beautiful spot I'd ever seen." Since this one was better than the last, I stopped the car, propped up my phone, figured out the timer, positioned myself in the frame, and took another selfie. I called Becky again to tell her about it.

I got back into the car, drove a bit farther into the park, and then guess what happened? That's right, I came across another, even more beautiful place. This one even had freshwater streams in it. Guess what I did? That's right. I stopped the car, propped my phone, figured out the timer, positioned myself in the frame, and took a selfie! When I called Becky, she said, "That's great, Honey. Why not tell me about all of it when you get home."

This went on all day. The deeper I went into the park, the more majestic the mountains and awe-inspiring the views became. I now have 500 selfies of me "in the most beautiful spot I've ever been to."

As I drove away from the park and as the sun went down, I gave God thanks for the day. Then I had a thought that I believe came from the Holy Spirit. I heard a voice in my head, which wasn't Wes, say, "This day is the way God's love is for you. Just as soon as you think you have discovered 'the most beautiful experience' of God's love, there's even more."

My prayer since that day has been to experience more of God's love in my life. Each time I stop and catch a glimpse of

God's love, and I think it may just be the best thing I've ever seen before, I wonder, "Could this be any better? Could there ever be more?" The answer from the Bible is a resounding yes!

In Ephesians 3:19, Paul prayed that all of God's children would see that there is always *more-ness* in the heart of God: "May you experience the love of Christ, though it is too great to understand fully. Then you will be made complete with all the fullness of life and power that comes from God." This love was beyond my human comprehension. When it came to God's love, there was always more. Paul knew that, as God's children experienced more and more of their lives in the light of this majestic love, they would "be made complete with all the fullness of life and power that comes from God." That sounded good to me. I had lived so long on empty that I was drawn to the thought of a reservoir of inner strength from outside my own limited resources.

I began to see God's love, not as a landmark I would visit once and take a quick selfie in front of, but as something I could revel in every single day. God's love was as vast as creation itself. There was always *more-ness* in the heart of God! This meant that I had lots *more* to discover; in my new, growing faith, I did not want to slip back into trying to earn the moreness of God's love. I had hit dead end after dead end trying to force my own spiritual maturity. With Bonnie's help, I began to search for new ways to approach a life-sustaining way of encountering more of God's love. Like the changes I had begun to experience, this change did not involve me *doing more* for God. To receive more of God's love, I needed to *do* less and *be* more.

Bonnie explained that my *being* with God is a choice that God empowers me to make. My *doing* is an outward sign of the inward grace of God that fills my being. She said, "Being is a priority and a necessity, for no matter what I do, it comes out of my being. We can't do anything until we decide who we're going to be! Otherwise, we tend to do what we want others to think we are"

I soon made the connection that Bonnie's priority for me to *be* before *doing* could be found in Jesus' word *abide* (see John 15 NRSV). Excitedly, I read that passage in John several times.

Abiding in Love

On the last night of his earthly ministry, Jesus taught his disciples about abiding. The shadow of the cross loomed larger by the minute, and he needed to impart some important concepts. Right before Jesus was betrayed, crucified, buried, and raised from the dead, he gathered with his disciples. During this night, he washed their feet, introduced what we know as the Lord's Supper, prayed for them, and gave them an analogy of a vine and branches.

In the Bible, the vine was often used by the prophets as a picture of Israel. Jesus added to this meaning by calling himself "the true grapevine." Those who belonged to Jesus were now God's chosen people. They were COGPOWs. This made sense to me.

Just as I might nurture a plant to help it grow, I could grow in my being by taking time to be with Jesus (my true vine). Jesus explained that abiding meant to remain intimately connected:

> I am the true grapevine, and my Father is the gardener. He cuts off every branch of mine that doesn't produce fruit, and he prunes the branches that do

bear fruit so they will produce even more. You have already been pruned and purified by the message I have given you. Remain in me, and I will remain in you. For a branch cannot produce fruit if it is severed from the vine, and you cannot be fruitful unless you remain in me.

Yes, I am the vine; you are the branches. Those who remain in me, and I in them, will produce much fruit. For apart from me you can do nothing. Anyone who does not remain in me is thrown away like a useless branch and withers. Such branches are gathered into a pile to be burned. But if you remain in me and my words remain in you, you may ask for anything you want, and it will be granted! When you produce much fruit, you are my true disciples. This brings great glory to my Father. John 15:1-8 (NLT; in the NRSV, "remain" is rendered as "abide")

In Jesus' analogy, Jesus is the vine, God is the gardener, and those who follow Jesus are the branches. Branches could produce fruit only when they were connected to the vine. Any branch that tried to go it alone wouldn't last long. Soon, cut off from life, they would be good for nothing except kindling for a fire.

These were sobering words from Jesus, and while some biblical scholars think Jesus may have been referring to the eventual judgment of Israel, many others (whom I tend to agree with) think this is best understood, not as a future consequence, but as the simple obvious result of what happens if we cut ourselves off from the very Source of life.

For "the Spirit of the living God" to continually "fall afresh on me" meant a lifelong prayer of asking God to "fill me." I had already learned the hard way that relying on my own resources was a dead end.

God, our Creator and Gardener in Jesus' teaching, had designed life this way. God planned for us to stay connected to the vine so that we could bear fruit. I felt a deep desire inside of me. I wanted to live a fruitful life.

To continue to experience the spectacular beauty of God's love meant that I needed to cooperate with God and position my life in the way The Gardener designed. This discovery took me back to my Papaw Olds' life and his example.

My Papaw Olds was a faithful farmer in Northern Kentucky, spending sixty-five years working one farm. He worked long hours every day but Sunday. When it was dark and others were sleeping, he got up early to milk the cows. He went out late to check the crops. As long as I live, I'll never forget his huge, strong, rough hands.

One Sunday, a pretentious young preacher came to my Papaw's farm for lunch after a worship service. After lunch, he and Papaw went outside. Standing in silence at the fence line overlooking the farm, the preacher surveyed the well-kept barns, silos, and neatly lined crops on the Kentucky hills. The preacher said: "Mr. Olds, God sure has given you a great piece of land here." To that, Papaw replied: "Yes the Lord did, but you should have seen this place when God had it all to himself!" Papaw was fruitful because he was faithful.

To me, this is what Jesus was saying about abiding. To abide was to remain with God. I noticed that, in the New Living

Translation, Jesus used the word *remain* seven times in the first eight verses alone and three more times in the next passage. To *remain* means to dwell in place and to abide. The call of Jesus for me was clear. Once again, I looked to Bonnie for help on where to start.

Bonnie worked with me to apply this concept of abiding to the regular, hectic, self-induced chaos that was my life. Now late in my third year of meeting with Bonnie, she helped me put into practice a new daily schedule for my week that included a whole day to abide called *Sabbath*.

Bonnie gave me permission to block one day a week, usually a Friday, for my Sabbath day. At first, I protested because, in my mind, I was too important. I was always on call, and *emergencies* kept me busy. She quickly defeated this straw-man argument of mine by having me understand the true definition of an emergency. An emergency was not that I didn't finish my sermon during my allotted study times; that was a time-management issue, not an emergency. An emergency was not that someone wanted me to do something for them or even visit them in the hospital; those could usually be done other times. As Bonnie helped narrow the definition of an *emergency* to people dying or nearly so, my schedule on Fridays suddenly opened up.

Soon, it became my favorite day of the week. Practically speaking, here's what that day involved. On that morning, I slept in and then leisurely spent time with God until mid-afternoon. Sometimes this involved listening to worship music, walking, listening to sermons, reading a book on the spiritual life, or engaging with the Bible.

After that, I'd pick up my son early in the afternoon to spend time with him. This was a highlight in my life during those difficult years. Both Caleb and I remember our first Father-Son date. We went to the Woodford County Railroad Yard and, for hours, we played together on real trains. Then we went home and played Thomas the Tank Engine with his wooden train collection. We had tons of fun!

Little did I know the blessing of that day. Our Father-Son dates on Fridays continued almost every week from preschool until the week Caleb left for college. On the rare occasion we missed one, we always made it up quickly. When he was younger, we would go to a park and play. When he was in middle school, it was to the library to each get new books, and then hours playing video games together. In high school, we simply went to Chili's! I didn't do everything right as a dad, but thanks to Bonnie and later other mentors, I enjoyed over 750 Friday afternoons with my amazing son. The weekly time to just delight in Caleb's life reminded me of God's love for me. Caleb may have taught me more about God's love than any other person, even my own parents.

Bonnie also helped me establish Date Night with my wife on Friday evenings. At the time, our marriage was in trouble following our compounded losses and my immature reactions. Becky and I met together many times with Bonnie during this season, and she helped us set boundaries for date night. We were not to try to solve anything. We were to love each other as fellow COGPOWs, share our feelings, and listen to one another. This practice helped us begin to rebuild our trust and friendship with one another. This practice has continued over the last twenty years and counting!

While Fridays became the highlight of my week, they were not easy to pull off. My life was busy. To carve out a whole day to seemingly *do nothing* was at first hard for me. As a pastor, I was on call for emergencies throughout the week, so this meant pre-planning a day in which my staff and collogues knew I would be unavailable. They would need to cover. It meant I had to leave things undone for a time. It ultimately meant that I had to trust God with my life and vocation. This seemed silly to write as a pastor, but the truth was, I needed to re-entrust Jesus with his own church!

The result was life-giving. Jesus was right. *Abiding* bears fruit, and pruning bears even more fruit. For a monumental example, I didn't need to look any further than my marriage. Whereas threats of divorce were once shouted in anger at each other, now we were approaching our third decade of a marriage that was healthy and life-giving. Peace, kindness, gentleness, joy, and love now filled our relationship most days.

This was what was noticeable and seen. But there was a deeper work of God in my life taking place through abiding. Not only was I loving God, but I have become a student of Sabbath and now joyfully share it with others whenever I can pass on the benefits of this practice.

From Performance Plan to Treasured Possession

The original story of the exodus began to resonate for me as it never had before. In many ways, the story of the Israelites felt very similar to my own struggle to move from excessive doing to resting in God's favor.

In the book of Exodus, God rescues the Israelite people from four hundred years of slavery in Egypt. For generations, God's chosen people were not human beings but human doers. They were *hands*, units of work, people tragically forced to live by *chronos* time, watching minutes tick by, day after day. As slaves, they were among history's saddest examples of life on the *performance plan*. Although the Israelites were forced, this was like my story when I lived for the approval of others instead of pleasing the heart of God.

During the time of their enslavement, the Egyptian calendar was made up of 36 ten-day weeks called *decans*. In Egypt, a year was 36 weeks x 10 days per week equaling 360 days. Five days were added to match a solar-based time. This was their existence: They had to work ten days, then ten more, then ten more . . . for the whole year! They had no day off. Ever. No time for worship. No time to rest. No time for relationships. This was the schedule of slavery! Constant pressure. Constant work. I could relate in my own life to the constant pressure to perform.[18]

It was no wonder then, that, as God delivered these weary Israelites, God's intimate care extended even to their schedules. Wilderness time was perhaps more than anything *break* time, time to break free of the rigorous schedule they were used to and time to cultivate relationships with God and each other. Once they were Pharaoh's slaves, but now they were called by God a "treasured possession" (Deut 14:2 NRSV). God was helping the people discover that they were more than just their usefulness. They were beloved by God. They were COGPOWs.

18   Anne-Sophie von Bomhard, *The Egyptian Calendar: A Work for Eternity* (London, UK: Periplus, 1999), 51.

Because the Israelites were used to receiving commands and orders, to bless them in a way they could comprehend, God gave them ten commandments to live by. But these orders came from a *far different motivation* than their experience of human masters and rulers. God gave these commands, not to exploit their labor, but so that they could experience the Lord's love and learn to connect relationally with God and one another. In John's Gospel, Jesus too gave commandments to his disciples so that, "joy may be in you and your joy may be complete" (John 15:11 NRSV).

The same was true for me. I felt God giving me the command of Sabbath for my good, so that I could experience more of God's grace in my life. God's commands were to help me abide, so I could experience more of God. In the past, I had always viewed God's commandments as more rules to follow to earn God's love. I was slowly starting to see that even God's commands were invitations to abide.

I saw now that this order of love was reflected in the order of the Ten Commandments itself. The first three of the Ten Commandments were all about how we are created to relate to God. We were to keep God in first place in our lives, not worship idols, and never use the name of the Lord in vain. These were *vertical* laws for how we love God.

The last six commands were about how we were to relate to one another. These were the *horizontal* laws. We were to honor our parents, not murder, not commit adultery, not steal, not give false witness, and we were not to crave and covet another persons' stuff.

The transition command between our relationship with God and our relationship with others was the fourth of "God's top ten list": keeping the Sabbath. This diagram from the work of Dr. Timothy Valentino helped me understand this concept:[19]

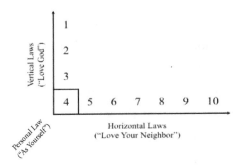

I cannot help but wonder if the ancient practice of *ceasing* for rest was one of God's first introductions to the Israelites of their new identity as COGPOWs. To live into their new identity, they were to stop their work, so they had time to be. All the way back in this time, God was communicating what Bonnie was telling me: Being comes before doing.

As a COGPOW, God empowered me to have dominion over my life and all God has entrusted to me. Continually living in this freedom involved continually creating space to be alone with God. There, in the presence of God, I was coronated anew as king of my village. In the quietness of prayer, I could better listen in on what the villagers were saying. In the space Sabbath created, God gave me an opportunity to retrain my Smurfs or exile them from my village.

19 Timothy R. Valentino, "Artistry and Architecture in the Fourth Commandment: New Proposals on the Context, Structure, and Beauty of Israel's Sabbath Law," *Evangelical Journal* 33, no. 2 (2015): 49-69.

Loving Myself

These times of quiet and rest have not always been easy. I'll be honest and let you know that as soon as you try this practice, new challenges appear that you must face with your friend and guide, Jesus.

The first challenge for me was simply stopping the busyness. Yet that's not the only resistance I've faced in this practice. A second challenge was even more perplexing; sometimes, it was not easy to be alone with my thoughts. When I was quiet, I did not always like what the village had to say, as I tried to listen in and abide in Jesus. The conversation in the village revealed places where I was limiting God's grace and my freedom of living as a COGPOW. It was easier in the short term to stay busy, so that the needs of these Smurfs could be drowned out by the noise of daily life.

Through the practice of weekly Sabbath, as well as times of quiet throughout my week, I had the time to listen to the village meeting taking place in my soul. I was sometimes shocked at what I heard! Getting to know myself, including my less-desirable voices and insecurities, was at times frightening.

Bonnie explained that this was common. "People can be homesick when they are with themselves, because they haven't made a home with the Lord in themselves," she said. Over time, she assured me, God's grace will fill me to the place where I can enjoy my own company, value myself, be honest with myself, and delight in being me. As I lived into my identity as a COG-POW, Bonnie assured me that I would grow more and more at ease in my own company. When I discovered something troubling in my village, I could invite God again to "search me" and "know me," and we could handle it together.

Several years later, abiding in Sabbath helped reveal an additional, elusive Smurf hiding out in my village. I named him Shadow Smurf, for he likes to stay in the dark. Shadow Smurf is fear. Shadow Smurf operates only in fear. He likes to say things to scare me. He always has the worst-case scenario in mind and says it. In many ways, he may have been the impetus for Abandonment Smurf, Anger Smurf, and Anxiety Smurf. He sometimes enrolls Anxiety Smurf and Anger Smurf in his schemes. When Shadow Smurf joins with Anxiety Smurf, they together begin to raise questions like "what if . . .," which provoke worry. When Shadow Smurf joins with Anger Smurf, they bully me: "Wes, you'll never get it together . . . why can't you figure this out yet . . . you blew it . . ., you didn't do your best."

Shadow Smurf made my mind a dangerous neighborhood and made my village hide in terror. When I first found Shadow Smurf, I wished for a chaperone to keep me safe. I found one in another counselor's office. I found this Smurf with the help of my new counselor named David. He helped expose Shadow Smurf one day by asking me to reveal my self-talk at a time I was having conflict with a close friend. Shadow Smurf couldn't resist the temptation to whisper his venom. I quoted him to David.

When I finished, David said, "Wow, Wes, would you ever say that to another person?"

"Never," I replied. "Not even to an enemy."

His instructions were simple: "Then never say that to yourself!"

It was the same rule that Bonnie had put in place: COG-POWs don't abuse COGPOWs, either themselves or others. Instead, COGPOWs operate out of the security of being loved. I am loved, Bonnie said repeatedly, because God loves me. That was it. Nothing could separate me from God's love.

Healing for my Shadow Smurf was incremental until Fall 2013. Following an intense season of ministry, I took ten days off and went on a road trip by myself. My wife and son were busy with work and school, and they knew I was weary, so they urged me to go and have some fun. Since I enjoy history, I rented a car and drove to historical sites all over the Southeast. I also stopped and saw some family and friends along the way.

God used the dozens of hours of drive-time, the visits to museums, and hiking around National Parks to bless me with the gift of divine love. The silence provided lots of time to pray. I wasn't expecting, hoping for, or planning any spiritual awakening, but God had other plans. As each day passed, I began to have an increasing sense of God's love for me. The very thought of God's *more-ness* filled me with increasing joy. I played worship music and sang praises to God until I was hoarse. I marveled at God's creation as I drove and saw different mountains and terrains. I listened to huge chunks of the Bible and was captivated by the story of God again. Best of all, I started thinking good thoughts, God's thoughts, about me. When my failures came to mind, I gave thanks to God for God's goodness and even managed to laugh at myself a few times. Often, my eyes filled with tears just considering the grace and mercy God had given to me. For the first time in a long time, I was not afraid.

The night before I returned home, I wrote my wife and son letters of gratitude for who they are and how God had blessed me through their love. They both commented that I was different and more relaxed. My then fourteen-year-old truthteller son said, "Dad, you sure seem a lot happier." I went back to see my counselor David a few days later, and his first question was, "So, how was your trip?" "Incredible," I said. "For the first time in a very long time, maybe since I was a child, I enjoyed being with me!" David said something I'll never forget: "That's a huge step of growth because, if you think about it, *you are with you* a lot!" I remembered that, years earlier, Bonnie had told me the same thing. I was starting to see that my renewed friendship with God was filling me with love enough to be friends with myself. I was no longer afraid to be with me.

In the coming years, I began to filter what was said in the village and season those comments with gentleness and kindness. My friend and partner in ministry, Jorge, even now asks me weekly: "Are you bullying yourself in any way?" Shadow Smurf disappears as soon as this question is asked. He simply can't stand light! When I live in the present, not in the world of *what if*, I've found God's peace to be possible inside of my mind and soul.

Five years after my surprisingly enjoyable road trip, I was blessed by my church with a four-month sabbatical. This included opportunities for even more extended times of quiet and prayer and more healing for Shadow Smurf. During this time, another supernatural encounter with God changed my thinking forever.

I was used to receiving dozens of texts and emails a day. Each message arrived with the sound of a little *ding* on my phone. During my sabbatical, however, no one contacted me except a small group of family and friends. I was nobody's pastor. All my responsibilities were cared for by a team of gifted leaders. To my surprise, I started missing being needed all the time. Since I was accustomed to looking at my phone, I set my alerts to ding several times a day with this message: "Wes, you are the beloved of God." It was a helpful exercise. I would hear the common ding, and like the proverbial Pavlov's dog, I was conditioned to pick up my phone. Instead of a new thing to do, I was reminded of my being: COGPOW.

After several weeks of this, I was on a walk in another National Park one afternoon when the Holy Spirit prompted me to look down. "What do you see?" God's Spirit seemed to ask. I looked down and saw my shadow in front of me on the path. God impressed these words on my mind: "Wes, your Shadow is now in front of you. You won't be ambushed anymore if you let me shine my light into your soul." Shadow Smurf lost his power that day.

Shadow Smurf's greatest power over my life was found in surprising me with ambushes of what if's. Bonnie had encouraged me fifteen years earlier to "live in the now." Jesus lives in "the now." He described himself seven times in the Gospel of John by saying, "I am . . ." Bonnie anchored her encouragement in the promise that God's perfect love drives out fear. She suggested I adopt a new thought pattern like this: "When you are afraid, remind yourself as a COGPOW: God has perfect love for me. God has a future for me that is good, and I do not need to fear the future."

Living as a COGPOW meant discovering new ways of being filled with God's love. It was God's love that had healed Anxiety Smurf, Anger Smurf, Abandonment Smurf, and now Shadow Smurf. Next, God's love revealed a new way of loving other people. As a confident COGPOW, God could transform my relationships. God could even use me to share the love that I had received.

"The Late Wes Olds" had found new life!

CHAPTER FIVE:
THE ORDER OF LOVE

Spirit of the living God, fall afresh on me.
Melt me, Mold me, Fill me, Use me.

One of Bonnie's favorite images each week in our meetings was that of God smiling. Whenever she described pleasing the heart of God, she smiled herself as she imagined God, our Father, smiling over us. The memory of her joyful grin and boisterous laugh are thankfully impressed in my soul. Even after a recent phone call regarding this book, she sent me a message that concluded with how it "put a smile on her face" to hear my voice. She lives into her nickname of *COGPOW Mama*.

Most important, in those critical meetings I had with her years ago, she modeled her own counsel of a COGPOW gracing the life of another COGPOW. I think it was her love and encouragement for me that made the most impact on me. In

those years when I felt like the world's greatest failure, I encountered a living expression of God's grace in her presence.
Her example gave me a new prayer for my own life: Spirit of
the Living God, fall afresh on me. *Use me.*

As a COGPOW, Bonnie taught, God has blessed and
graced my life. As I continued to discover how to live in this
grace, God could also use me to help others. "God is smiling,"
she said, whenever I value myself by claiming the value God has
given me, and then freely give that gift to others. God's plan for
me was not to take on the burdens of the world. Jesus already
did that. Yet in that gift, I was empowered to be a grace-giver
to transform the lives of people in my life. As a COGPOW, I
had been given blessings. I could use them to make a difference
in my relationships with others.

As I claimed my own power and strength, God gave me
newfound maturity in my relationships with others. God's love
gave me a breakthrough, not only in my own identity, but by
changing the way I saw other people as fellow COGPOWs.
They, like me, needed grace, forgiveness, and encouragement
to live to please the heart of God. While all these concepts
seemed spot-on and exciting, living these out in my relationships was going to involve yet another change in my life.

A Nursery of Raccoons

Growing up in Kentucky, one of the scariest critters I
would occasionally encounter as a child playing in the woods
was a raccoon. When my friends and I found ourselves in the
presence of one or more rabid raccoons, we were terrified!
These critters may look nice and cuddly, but in the wild they

are mean and will bite. We had two choices in those moments face-to-face with danger: Either fight with screams and sticks until they ran away, or choose flight, and run for our lives!

Fight or flight: These two options were not just my rules for encountering raccoons. Sadly, these two mantras also served as my playbook for handling relationship difficulties. Written boldly on the Wall of my soul were these two options for relational pain, and only these two. This lasted well beyond my childhood and into adulthood. I was both emotionally hyper-sensitive and emotionally immature.

Here was a typical experience: When a person I was with was angry, sad, hurting, frustrated, weary, unsure, opinionated, or any other strong emotion I deemed negative, I was filled with fear. Almost immediately, I would then *catch* their misery and take it upon myself. It was like holding a rabid raccoon. Often, the person who handed me their raccoon of rage, disappointment, or loss felt momentarily better, for they found a place to set their pain down for a time . . . with me! The problem was that rabid raccoons don't want to be held; when it's attempted, they scratch and claw and bite their way to freedom. I would endure patiently as long as possible, but chances were high that, when I was with an angry person, I too was soon angry. In that moment, it was time to either fight with that person and win or choose flight and run! If I was going to help other COGPOWs, I had to learn to stop catching and holding their raccoons.

The Order of Love: Loving Neighbors

Out of the overflow of loving God and God pouring love into my life, Bonnie suggested that a new resource was available to me for relating to others, something Jesus had promised would come to me through the Holy Spirit as "living water," a source that would never run dry. With the overflow of God's love pouring into my life, new possibilities suddenly emerged for loving others that went far beyond "fight or flight." Bonnie introduced to me ways that God could "use me" (even me!) to share grace with others. These new rules replaced the *raccoon catching* that was making me feel exhausted and weary. Bonnie's "new rules" on relationships:

- Someone else's pain doesn't need to be mine. Know that I cannot fix what I did not break.

- When others are in need, I am to be faithful to God, do what I can, and move on with a clean conscience.

- I am not responsible for another human being's thoughts, feelings, actions, or conditions. I am responsible for mine.

- I can help people without becoming their caretakers. They must be responsible for themselves.

- Who other people are does not determine my reactions or responses. I am free! I control myself.

Just hearing these rules felt like water to a parched soul. I was so tired of trying to fix everyone! As a pastor of a struggling church, the cofounder of a city-wide ministry to persons who were homeless, a family member, a friend, a son, a father, and a husband, I couldn't keep holding everyone else's raccoons. I had my own to deal with.

Yet every night, I went home with a herd of raccoons, which, ironically, animal experts call a *nursery*. That's right, a bunch of lions is called a *pride*, a group of elephants is aptly named a *parade*, and if you get a few dozen alligators together, they are called a *congregation*. (As a pastor, I'm going to leave that alone.) A gathering of raccoons, however, is a *nursery*.

How I related to the *nursery* of others' emotions and my own needed to change. I wish I could tell you that I immediately was healed of my relational immaturity, and that I instantly had the power to love my neighbors. Sadly, this was not the case.

Not only did I need to grow up in my relationship with God and my relationship with myself. I also needed new formulas for the ways I related to others. I needed a new story, not based in the fears of my Shadow Smurf, but grounded in the freedom and security of my identity as a COGPOW. As I began to know who I was in relationship with God and in my relationship with myself, I also needed to discover who I was in *relationship with others*.

As I have shared, relationships for me are complicated. One of my favorite poems goes like this:

> To live above with those we love, well, that will be glory.

> To live below with those we know, well, that's another story.[20]

The story of my relational world when I first met Bonnie was one full of pain. At the time, both my wife Becky and I were reeling from the home invasion and later, our son Daniel's

---

20 Adapted from the poem as presented in Christopher J.H. Wright, *Cultivating the Fruit of the Spirit: Growing in Christlikeness* (Downers Grove, IL: InterVarsity Press, 2017). 80.

death. Following these events, each of us retreated into our own agony. We each had several nurseries of *raccoons* we were trying to manage. For Becky, this pain manifested in grief that eventually gave way to depression. As you know, my grief spurred a furious anger with God, myself, and anyone who might threaten my fragile remains of self-worth. Despite our difficulties, we found common ground in that we both wanted to offer our very best to our eldest son, Caleb, who was fast approaching his fourth birthday. That was when God's grace began to write a new story in our relationship as husband and wife.

Loving Our First Neighbor

At first, Becky refused to join me in counseling. I don't blame her. I'm sure the thought of spending another hour with me was less than inviting. Also at the time, Becky was working as a licensed marriage and family therapist, counseling children with emotional and behavioral disabilities. With her stellar experience, education, and credentials, Becky reasoned, she knew what to do and didn't need additional help.

Despite her reluctance, I kept gently inviting Becky to join me. Thankfully, after several months of inviting, she eventually agreed to see Bonnie with me for one session. Watching our interactions in that first meeting, Bonnie advised us to see her individually for a season. It was clear to all that we needed help. We agreed to her plan. In her one-on-one sessions with Bonnie, Becky quickly discovered that counselors need counselors just as much as anyone else, and she now says, "if not more." I am forever grateful for Becky's decision to seek help with me.

In addition to discovering our God-given worth as beloved children, Bonnie helped us begin to love one another as "our first neighbor." Some weeks, we each saw Bonnie individually and then together, to implement more new rules on our souls' walls. These new rules dealt with how we loved each other, and unlike our old graffiti of blame and isolation, they were filled with grace and pleased the heart of God. They blessed us to be a blessing for each other. One of Bonnie's mantras to both of us during this time was, "Solve the problem, don't be the problem. Together, with God, you can deal with whatever comes."

With our blessing, Bonnie enlisted her husband Ron as one of our prayer partners. After several months, Becky and I began to separate our shared trauma and grief as "the problem" and begin to walk through the valley of the shadow of death together as friends. As the fighting lessoned, it was honestly good to have each other to lean on again.

We soon developed additional new rules. We made a rule for our family: "Everyone in our household is a COGPOW. COGPOWs love other COGPOWs." We began to honor one another in that way. We put this new rule on the refrigerator as a constant reminder. To live this out, we began family meals together. At that nightly meeting around the kitchen table, we shared what in the day had made us happy and what made us sad. This led to new opportunities to listen to and encourage one another. We also prayed with and for each other, often with our son Caleb leading us in singing "Johnny Appleseed" at the top of our lungs as a blessing over the food.

This chorus of gratitude was based on the life of American folk hero John Chapman, who (legend has it) once wandered the Ohio Valley preaching the Bible, giving medicine to the sick, and distributing apple seeds. Our family song-of-blessing took place no matter where we were: At home, friends' homes, and even when we were out to eat. In more than one fancy (and quiet) restaurant, when the food came, Caleb announced, "Let's pray!" Becky and I would look and wink at one another with joyful anticipation, join hands, and then our family song broke through the surrounding hush. We sang:

Oh, the Lord's been good to me!

> And so, I thank the Lord, for giving me the things I need,

> The sun and the rain,

> and the apple seed.

> The Lord's been good to me![21]

With shared gratitude for the Lord's goodness in our lives and resting in our own COGPOW identities, we began to love one another as fellow Children of God Persons of Worth. It was good to laugh again. I think it put a smile on God's face, too!

Bonnie's additional rules included identifying and finding ways to honor our first neighbors; family or close friends who lived closest to us and knew us most and best. She then helped us name our secondary neighbors; family that included our friends and mentors. Next, we prioritized and named our spiritual family, our community relationships, and those in the world God had put along our path. This was the beginning of new discoveries about loving others as COGPOWs. For our

---

21   "Johnny Appleseed." This widely known and often-quoted nursery rhyme appears to be in public domain.

living-breathing-model of what those relationships looked like, we had a perfect guide, Jesus, to show us the way.

The First Crisis

Jesus teaches a great deal on relationships, beginning by modeling for us that life is not a solo sport. Instead, life is a team game. Early in his public ministry, Jesus invited others to join him in life and ministry. There were no *free-agent* followers of Jesus in the Gospels. God made us for community. Even God lives in community as Father, Son, and Holy Spirit.

Interestingly, the first crisis in the Bible was not a moral failure. It was a relational problem. After repeatedly celebrating each act of creation by saying, "It is good!" Genesis 2:18 interrupts the relishing with this sobering commentary: God says, "It is not good for the human to be alone" (my version). When God says something is "not good," we need to pay attention, because it means things are not good!

In my case, God never intended for me to try to deal by myself with the grief over the loss of my son or the guilt over the attack on my family. The common platitude, "God will never give you more than you can handle," is not in the Bible. It is a misquote of a verse dealing with temptation not being more than we can bear without God's help (see 1 Cor 10:13). Temptation is far different than trauma, loss, or heartache. Even temptation is not to be resisted alone, but with God's enduring presence and unlimited power.

Scripture calls us to bear one another's burdens, to pray for one another, to comfort one another, to encourage one another, and dozens of more *one-another's*. This call to community was one of Jesus' final teachings and commands for his disciples before facing the cross.

Ya'll and You'se-guys

I had liked to view loving God and abiding as something I did when I was alone. But I soon realized that Jesus taught that abiding continues when I am with others. In fact, the entire section of Scripture in which Jesus teaches about abiding is in the plural tense. This means that if Jesus were from Kentucky, he'd be saying "ya'll" or, if he was from New Jersey, he would say, "you'se guys." When Jesus said "you," it was directed at the whole group of disciples. Jesus was saying, "You all are the branches, abide in me." Have you ever seen a tree with only one branch?

We have been designed to live life connected to Jesus and connected to other Jesus-followers. Jesus' teaching continues and specifically addresses how we should relate to one another. To help me grasp Jesus' words, I added *all* to each time Jesus included our relationships with others.

> I have loved you [all] even as the Father has loved me. Remain in my love. When you [all] obey my commandments, you [all] remain in my love, just as I obey my Father's commandments and remain in his love. I have told you [all] these things so that you [all] will be filled with my joy. Yes, your joy will overflow! (John 15:9-11)

Jesus' life illustrated just how far this love was willing to go for us and how we were to be a true neighbor to others. If I wanted to learn how to be in relationship with others, I needed first to draw example and strength from my place of abiding with Jesus.

Laying Down My Life

I knew that a willingness to "lay down one's life for one's friends" (John 15:13) has been known as the highest ideal of love in human history. Aristotle had named this virtue over three hundred years earlier, but Jesus was the first to put it into practice. Jesus died on a cross for those first disciples, for me, and for all of you reading this book. Jesus laid down his life in obedience to God for his friends. I discovered that, out of my abundance of being a COGPOW, Jesus was commanding me to follow his example. The more I asked God to "fill me," the more God would be able to "use me."

Remember, Jesus' whole image was one of a vineyard, not one lone vine trying to survive in isolation. In Jesus' teaching, those disciples who were bearing "much fruit" were bound in love with other people. I realized that I needed others to support and cultivate my own relationship with Jesus. At times, God the Gardener would use fellow friends of Jesus as instruments of cleansing and pruning. Fellow friends of Jesus helped me be a better friend of Jesus.

These friendships found their power through our humbly serving one another. To experience change in my relationships, I changed my approach. Instead of making another long to-do list like I used to, I decided that Jesus' life taught me to do one thing in order for me to love others well: to serve.

The night in which Jesus shared all those beautiful last words with his disciples began in a culturally awkward way. By the door in every residence in Jerusalem, especially during the busy travel season of Passover, there is a place for travelers to have their feet washed. Foot washing was not a ceremony; it was very practical. In the days before pavement, garbage collection, and sewer systems, travelers' feet would be covered in dust, manure, dirt (and worse) from the crowded streets. The servant of the household, the *lowliest* servant in status, would take the basin and towel and wash the feet of the guests coming in from the road. Also at this time, the custom was to recline as you ate, so your feet were near the face and food of the next guest. No stinky feet wanted!

This didn't happen in the Upper Room. No servant was present, and none of the disciples offered to do the task. Imagine this: One by one, the disciples entered the room, and they ignored the basin and the towel by the door. They didn't even wash their own feet before they took their seats at the table.

Finally, everyone had arrived and had taken their places at the table. Still, nobody had washed anyone's feet! It feels humorous to picture the disciples all around the table, waiting for Jesus to start the meal, cluelessly sitting with twenty-four stinking, filthy feet reclining "toes to nose" from disciple to disciple. Jesus seized this as a teaching moment: "So, he got up from the table, took off his robe, wrapped a towel around his waist, and poured water into a basin. Then he began to wash the disciples' feet, drying them with the towel he had around him" (John 13:4-5).

Earlier, John had said that Jesus loved his disciples, that he loved them until the end. This meant teaching them that the way to love others was to give their lives in service. By washing their feet, he showed them that the way to live life to the fullest was not through climbing up but through bending down. All of Jesus' teaching, his words on abiding, his command to love one another, the Last Supper, culminated with Jesus serving others for the glory of God.

In a world obsessed with *moving up*, how did Jesus continue to choose to stoop down? He did so in the security of his own COGPOW-ness! This became a model story for me to live out in my own relationships.

The apostle Paul said, "In your relationships with one another, have the same mindset as Christ Jesus" (Phil 2:5 NIV). This meant that, in my relationships with others, I needed to be facing *down*. It meant stooping to serve, giving up my rights for God's righteousness, and striving to serve and love not only people who were my family and friends but those whom nobody else wanted or saw.

My dad had modeled this in his life. He died in 2008 at the age of 62, after a twelve-year battle with cancer. To celebrate his life, we held two huge funeral services. Dad left a legacy as a loving husband and father, a prince of preachers, but best of all as a servant of God. The song we chose to have sung at the end of that emotional rollercoaster of services, right before his burial, was a mantra for his life:

> If I can help somebody as I travel along;
>
> If I can help somebody with a word or song,

If I can help somebody from doing wrong,

Then my living shall not be in vain.[22]

Out of gratitude for what Jesus had done in my life, in the security of my identity as a COGPOW, I needed to imitate Jesus. I've found that I can do this best in choosing humility. The word *humble* comes from the word *humus*. It means "from the dirt" or "down to earth." The Bible teaches that "God opposes the proud but gives grace to the humble" (Jas 4:6). Humility is a choice that positions our lives to receive more and more grace.

For much of my life, I had thought more about competition than about serving. This was true even when it came to my relationships with others. When I was a child in preschool, I wanted to be the *line leader*. When I was playing in band, I wanted to be *first-chair*. When I played football, I wanted to be *first-string*. When it came to leadership positions, I wanted to be voted class *president*. When it came to academics . . . well, honestly, I just wanted to pass. Overall, however, I wanted to be first! It wasn't until I discovered that I was given the identity as a COGPOW that these pursuits to find a gift that God had already given me began to be uncovered.

In 2011, I had an experience that brought this lesson to life. I had been serving as an associate pastor at Grace Church, where today I am privileged to serve as the Lead Pastor. At the time, Grace Church was the fastest growing of our worldwide connection of 32,000 churches. Dr. Jorge Acevedo, our Lead Pastor, was on a roll. God was using Jorge to write multiple books, host conferences, and speak to tens of thousands of pastors and leaders per year. He received multiple awards and was

22   Alma Bazel Androzzo, "If I Can Help Somebody" (1945).

on the cover of leadership magazines. Wherever I went, people asked: "Are you one of the pastors at Jorge's church? Do you get to work with Jorge?"

Now, the dirty secret of pastors is that many of us host an illness called *competition*. I seemingly had a doubly bad case. While Jorge has been and remains one of my closest friends for over three decades, I started getting a serious case of envy. It was bad. I started thinking, "Where's my book deal? Where's my speaking invitation?" Some voice in my village began torturing me with thoughts like, "Wes, you better find a way to get some fame and notoriety. You better find your way to be popular and influential."

On August 12, 2011, we became a video venue for a global leadership summit, hearing from some of the world's greatest leaders. For me that event was painful. A collection of my Smurfs joined together to criticize me day after day. They became louder and louder with statements like: "Wes, you should be there someday leading and speaking. Why aren't you? You must be failing in your ministry to be such a nobody. Maybe you need to leave Grace Church."

It was brutal.

At the end of the event, the last speaker talked about how God loves and uses broken people. He took a pot and broke it. We were each given pieces of broken pottery on our way in. He invited us to spend time taking our brokenness to God. That got my attention. I qualified as broken!

As I prayed, God once again searched me and knew my anxious ways. God revealed that the thoughts I had were harming me and that, once again, I was bullying myself. Then, in a surprising moment of prayer, God offered to take it away if I would trust God. First, I had to let go of my desire for accolades and applause from others. God impressed on me that I if I let go, I would get a new assignment that would satisfy my ambitious soul at last.

After a time in prayer surrendering my ambition, God gave me two words and the perfect assignment: *Be unknown*. That's right. *Be unknown*. At first, I thought I had misheard God! "Wes," God said, "Let go of your self-promotion and trust me. Nothing would put a smile on my face more than you simply imitating Jesus." I wrote those words on the broken piece of pottery. I carry it with me to this day. My assignment to put a smile on God's face became these words: "Wes, be unknown."

In that moment and in the coming weeks and years, a huge burden of pressure was lifted. I found Jesus' way was not nearly as heavy as my own. I discovered something else: There isn't a lot of competition in our world to be unknown. I could do that with ease! It took so much energy out of me to try to be noticed and in first place. A life of downward mobility was so much easier, so different that it was fun. Soon, my friend Jorge's success was something I could celebrate. I was free to be me. I no longer needed plaques with my name on them to validate my life. God's smile was rewarding enough. God's plan all along was to use me to bless others with all the love I had generously been given.

I have always been drawn to Jesus. His combination of security in his identity and the freedom with which he extended love fascinated me and drew me toward him even as a child. As

I reclaimed my identity as a COGPOW with childlike trust, I began to live in the security of being a COGPOW. I discovered that Jesus had a different way of defining success. The goal in his life was simply pleasing the heart of his Father, even in his relationships with others.

Instead of making himself powerful in the eyes of others, Jesus claimed the power given to him by his Father. In reading the biographies of Jesus, I claimed a new mantra for the way I was now free to serve others. I set it as a goal to "make others powerful" in God's love and found strength in the words of Henri Nouwen:

> Powerlessness and humility in the spiritual life do not refer to people who have no spine, who let everyone make decisions for them. They refer to people who are so deeply in love with Jesus that they are ready to follow him wherever he guides them, always trusting that with him, they will find life and find it abundantly.[23]

Over the last two decades, I have been discovering more of this life, and I find it is filled with both challenges and unspeakable joy. Bonnie helped me see that when we pray "use me," God gives us opportunities to share what we have been given. Bonnie called this concept "ripples."

Ripples of Grace

In every relationship, COGPOWs learn to *ripple* God's love. When you throw a rock in the center of a calm lake, the impact creates ripples that radiate, often dozens of yards away.

---

23   Henri Nouwen, *In the Name of Jesus* (New York, NY: Crossroad, 1992), 63-64.

The same is true with God's love. When God's grace impacts the soul of a person, the ripples extend farther than we can even see. As a COGPOW, I was to *ripple*.

As a COGPOW, I was uniquely called by God with the delightful assignment of "writing blessings on the walls of others' souls." In my one-on-one conversations with Bonnie, whenever I would complement Becky or another person about whom I had a good thought, she would ask: "Did you tell them? If you have a good thought, let it out!" I started trying this, and it stuck.

Randomly blessing others has become a fun, joyful, lifelong practice for me. On my best days, when I have a thought of gratitude for someone, I will often text them out of the blue and thank them, even if it was for a memory from long ago. Here's the motive behind this practice and why it was important to me in my recovery from others' esteem: The goal was not to gain a person's approval but simply to give God thanks! This puts a smile on the face of God, and it put a smile on my face as well. The role of a true COGPOW was to ripple the grace God toward others. My new rules for living and loving others were much better and more fun than the old messages of graffiti that once filled my wall!

As Bonnie described loving others through these ripples, she did so with a lightness of being that I longed to experience. When first I thought of loving others, I tended to feel overly responsible. Bonnie often replied with a rhetorical question that originated with her grandmother: "Wes, if God had meant for you to do it all, why did he make all these other people?"

Bonnie explained: "The purpose of life is to be faithful, to please God, to make ripples. God is in charge of the world. I must learn to trust that God is using other people to impact the world as well. I am not God, and God didn't make me God!"

In her coaching on loving others, Bonnie was planting seeds that would grow in my life over the next two decades. These all came together for me in a new way one day when a person with a nursery full of *raccoons* sought to ambush me with anger. Instead of fight or flee, I did something new.

Don't Hold Someone Else's Raccoon!

One day in late 2018, almost twelve years after my meetings with Bonnie drew to a close, a person came to me announcing, "Wes, I'm very, very frustrated with you! You and I need to talk right now!" I literally felt panic arising in my stomach and felt lightheaded. My fight-or-flight response was triggered. Yet God's power steadied me, and I got creative. Instead of running or gearing up for a verbal showdown, I imagined this person approaching me as if he were holding a nursery of rabid raccoons. I envisioned, as he started sharing his rage, that he was wanting to hand me a fictional, rabid raccoon.

Suddenly, a voice I can only attribute to God gave me a new possibility: "Wes, don't hold that raccoon! His anger is his. Don't pick it up!" Instead of becoming fused into the other person's emotional state, I stood confidently in my COG-POW-ness and said, "Yes, friend, please help me understand what has you so upset." I did not want ambush him or allow his problem to become my problem. My hope was to find the real problem and address it. In this way, I could live into my COG-POW-ness and serve this person. Instead of fighting or running away, I prayed that I could make him powerful in God's love.

During our meeting, I offered to listen to him, to learn about his raccoon, and to talk with him about what to do about it. I made sure I didn't pick it up but offered to pray with him. That meeting went unlike any other I had ever had. Like never before, I lived into the security of my COGPOW identity. The person's disapproval of me did not hurt. It was uncomfortable at times, but his opinion did not penetrate the forcefield of love that God had quietly been installing in me for the past dozen or more years. The person ended up in tears, confessing areas of his life that brought him constant pain and shame. I extended grace and resources to help him begin a new chapter. As a result, he called a counselor and began a new journey of healing with God. As he left my office, I did what Bonnie calls "a happy dance." I had put a smile on God's face, and my own too!

Since that day, not every painful encounter has gone perfectly by any means, but things have been different. By naming immature emotions and responses from others as *raccoons*, I've found this silly image to be helpful in beginning to create emotional boundaries for my soul.

Differentiation

Experts in family systems theory or psychology may aptly label this raccoon-metaphor as an expression of *differentiation*. Somehow, I never fully understood this concept until that day I met my angry person and did something new. Bonnie helped me begin a journey that continues to this day, where instead of fighting or fleeing, I can stay with someone in his or her anger, while not taking it upon myself. This is differentiation: The ability to stay close to people without becoming enmeshed in their emotions or behavior.

People with a high level of differentiation have their own beliefs, convictions, directions, goals, and values apart from the pressures around them. They can choose, before God, how they want to be without being controlled by the approval or disapproval of others. This had been one of the root causes of my pursuit of others' esteem and life on the performance plan.

Here is the good news of life as a COGPOW: We live to please the heart of God and are free to love and serve other people, regardless of their acceptance or approval of us. As a COGPOW, I can "be separate together" and know where I end and another person begins. In my discovery of this gift, I've found my inner dialogue while I am with a person may go something like this: "*I may not agree with you or you with me. Yet I can remain in relationship with you. I don't have to detach from you, reject you, avoid you, or criticize you to validate myself. God being my helper, I can be myself apart from you.*"

In reflecting on what caused me to run away from conflict or engage so intensely, I realized it was my own insecurity and fear. I was afraid that if I were around a person who votes a different way than I do or believes or behaves in a different way about issues, or reads the Bible a different way, or holds different convictions, that I might be threatened in some way. Worst of all, I could be rejected or abandoned.

To cope with this fear, my response in stressful relationships was often to run away, so that I could protect my fragile identity. As I have begun to live into my new security and confidence in God, I am more easily available for other people. I am no longer threatened by a difference of opinion. I wonder how our polarized world could be changed by simply discovering the power of differentiation found in living as a COGPOW. Imagine people of differing political and cultural convictions loving one another. For COGPOWs, this is not a fairy tale. It is possible. With the confidence of a COGPOW, new options appear. Instead of being filled with fear and looking to run or run over a person with an opposing view or emotion, I am discovering the power that God gives to COGPOWs to love others as COGPOWs, even those with whom I disagree.

I'm beginning to find that the Holy Spirit can give me the power and discernment to look behind the behavior of others. When I do, I don't just look at the problem but find the pain. One of my leadership coaches told me that, when I have trouble with someone, I don't need to get even, get away, get scared, or get mad. What I need to do is to get curious. I need to start with questions. I need to ask the Holy Spirit to help discern what deeper issue is going on with that person and possibly myself. How can I find out a person's story and how it is impacting him or her? He explained it to me this way: "Wes, the easiest way to lead a camel is the way it's already going." Since I love animal analogies, this one stuck.

Today, I'm learning to walk with people a little while, asking questions like, "Hey, I see you're quite upset and maybe angry, tell me a little more what's going on. I care about you." Sometimes, I can be a part of God's plan to ripple the grace

I have received and share it with another, even in trying moments. Jesus was a master at this in relationships. I recently discovered that in the four biographies of Jesus, he was recorded as asking 307 questions of people to probe more deeply into their souls. Simply listening was frequently the way Jesus loved others. I think this was why Jesus could have friendships with people across the social, political, religious, and cultural barriers of his time.

Jesus was able to befriend people who collaborated with the occupying Romans, as well as those who wanted to start a violent revolution. He loved the rich young man who came to him for advice on eternal life. He befriended a woman who was of a different racial and socioeconomic background. Jesus saw heroes like a Good Samaritan in groups of people whom other Jewish leaders despised. He once traveled to heal a crazed man who lived in the cemetery of an unclean region and healed the child of a local religious leader. He invited a well-esteemed Pharisee named Nicodemus to be born again, and he enjoyed meals with those the religious people labeled "notorious sinners." Jesus could party with the *scum* of the earth or go pray with the *select* of society. His disciples could come, and they could also go. What freedom!

Jesus could stay close to imperfect people due to the relationship he held most dear: his relationship with God, his perfect Father. It was an amazing discovery for my own healing from codependency that Jesus had this gift of COGPOW differentiation. Jesus was close to people, yet Jesus never let their approval, disapproval, agenda, or opinions distract him from his Heavenly Father's love for him or mission for his life. God's smile was his only goal.

I am living proof that, when a person experiences grace, one can start to feel safe and non-anxious. When a person feels loved, that person can receive the truths that set them free. This is the gift I received in Bonnie's office and the one I hope to offer you: You are a Child of God Person of Worth.

Playing Myself in the Story of Jesus

The first Christmas that I was meeting with Bonnie and discovering the joy of being a COGPOW, I was also the pastor of a small, struggling church. That year, our children's ministry team decided to put on a Christmas children's play. There had not been many children in that church for a long time, and now we had two dozen or more, including my son Caleb, who was in preschool and was, frankly, adorable. The play had been planned, and the parts were handed out.

I learned later that the leaders came to Caleb and asked what part he wanted in the Christmas play. They first asked, "Caleb, would you like to be a shepherd?" In disgust Caleb replied, "I'm not a shepherd, I'm Caleb." Okay, they said, "Would you be a wise man?" "No," said Caleb. "I am not a wise man. I'm Caleb." They offered him every part they could. Over and over, he said, "I'll be in the play, but I will be Caleb."

Sunday night came around and the church held its first Christmas play in over a decade. I was rushing around doing everything from trying to greet people to getting the lights and the stage lights and sound just right. It wasn't until the kids came out that I saw what was unfolding. On the stage were two kids dressed as Mary and Joseph huddled around a baby doll in a manger, some boys and girls dressed as wise men, and a few dressed as shepherds. Others were dressed as animals and even stars. Then, I saw my son Caleb come out and stand next to the manger. As a concerned father and pastor, my busyness halted, and I sat down to watch.

I'm glad I did not miss that moment. While all the other kids were in costumes, Caleb stood wearing his jeans and Thomas the Tank Engine T-shirt next to the kids in bathrobes. That's right: Caleb was playing himself in the Christmas play!

The Holy Spirit spoke to me in the midst of that busy time. "Wes," I sensed the Lord say, "I want to invite you to be a part of the Christmas story. Come just as you are. You don't have to dress up, play some part, or try so hard. Just be yourself. Come as you are and be with me."

It was the best Christmas pageant ever.

When I grow up, my prayer is to play myself in the story of Jesus. I think that will put a smile on God's face, and also on mine.

My prayer is the same for you. May you experience the blessing of living your life as God's beloved. God's grace and smile are available especially for you.

You are a COGPOW.

MEET THE AUTHORS

Wes Olds

Wes Olds is the Lead Pastor of Grace Church, a multisite congregation with three locations in Southwest Florida. He is a graduate of The University of Kentucky and Asbury Theological Seminary. Wes serves as a coach with Spiritual Leadership, Incorporated (SLI) and as a board member of the Southwest Florida Community Foundation. He is a recipient of the Lily Foundation Award for Clergy Renewal and co-author of the study series and book *A Grace-Full Life*.

Prior to coming to Grace Church, Wes began a multicultural, urban church called The Rock-La Roca United Methodist Church in Lexington, Kentucky. While there, he co-founded Lexington's chapter of "Room in the Inn," a city-wide ministry of hospitality and shelter for homeless men. Before that, Wes was a youth pastor at three United Methodist churches, an instructor at Asbury University, and writer for student ministry publications.

Wes is married to Becky, and they have one adult son named Caleb. Wes loves music, enjoys fishing, driving his Mustang, sports, and travel to historical sites with lots of plaques!

You can reach Wes Olds at 239-574-7161 or at info@ egracechurch.com.

Bonnie Crandall

Bonnie was born in Detroit, Michigan, the youngest of four daughters of a Methodist pastor. A BA in theater and music allowed her to work for many years in those fields in California, Arizona, Tennessee, and Kentucky. At age 48, she returned to graduate school and earned an MA in counseling, then finished out her major work life as a Licensed Clinical Counselor. She worked primarily with educators, doctors, and clergy (mind, body, spirit), which she sees as a neglected counseling group. She is also an impacting retreat leader and speaker.

Bonnie created a new counseling approach to self-imaging and wholeness she calls COGPOW. It stands for "Child of God Person of Worth." It combines biblical application with a restorative cognitive behavioral format. Believing each unique individual is loved, created, and valued by God, she affirms the worth of each person. She also applies the healing power of laughter and joy, sprinkled with words of affirmation and possibilities for all. A Christian and lifelong member of The United Methodist Church, her eternal desire is to hear "Well done, good and faithful servant."

She is blessed with a supportive husband, Ron; two fine sons, Matthew and Joshua; a delightful daughter-in-law, Jennifer; and two grandchildren, Julia and Jordan. Her greatest blessing was being open to the "still small voice" of God, as together they formulated this new counseling approach based on "COGPOW."

Bonnie Crandall is available for talks, workshops, or counseling. Counselors wanting additional information on the COGPOW method can reach her at COGPOWinfo@gmail.com.